GW00363359

KAS
9

SUCCESSFUL SEA ANGLING

SUCCESSFUL SEA ANGLING

by

DAVID CARL FORBES

With illustrations by the author

DAVID & CHARLES
NEWTON ABBOT

ISBN 0 7153 5116 8

To Maureen, who provides the final pleasure—
invariably grilled!

Set in eleven on thirteen point Baskerville
and printed in Great Britain
by Clarke Doble & Brendon Limited Plymouth
for David & Charles (Publishers) Limited
South Devon House Newton Abbot Devon

CONTENTS

LIST OF ILLUSTRATIONS

INTRODUCTION

The term fishing is something of a generalisation, for no other pastime contains within itself so many aspects embracing so many different facets, some so far divorced from each other in style as to be hardly comparable. And yet, despite this variance of styles and techniques, there is a special cameraderie among anglers, almost masonic, established immediately it is known that the other man fishes. It contributes much to the fascination of angling.

The non-angler is often surprised to discover that angling is the largest participant pastime in the country, and wonders what on earth anglers find in angling. Conversely, anglers wonder why on earth there are such people as non-anglers, and constantly try to remedy the situation. *They* are not at all surprised at the great enthusiasm for catching fish.

In a world where so little is left entirely to the whim of the individual, fortunately there is still fishing. There are virtually no rules, no times to start or to finish, very little that is truly predictable, much that is speculation, and great scope for ingenuity. The words *always* and *never* do not apply in angling.

It is hardly surprising that in recent years there has been such a great increase of interest in sea fishing. There are no frontiers or limitations to the sport to be found in the sea, and one takes as much from sea fishing as one puts into it. The man content to lay back in a chair, with rod pointing to the sky and fishing for itself, enjoys the sun and the sounds of the sea on the shingle, and, when he has done, he packs his rod and is happy with a brace of flounders. Another man may go afloat in search of winter cod, or clamber over difficult rock faces to find his sport in a more rugged environment. And then, perhaps, when the fish do not come, there is compensation in a sense of Spartan achievement.

There is beachcasting, with the whir of the reel in a cast which is a skill in itself, spinning along the rocks for bass, drifting, or legering in deep water for skate; and if one aspect is too tough or too dull, then you choose another until the sea provides the reward. And, invariably, that which you do catch is very good to eat. Those who know only frozen food have never tasted *real* fish!

Of all the diversifications to be found in angling in general, none are so wide as those to be found in sea angling in particular. For here there is something for everyone, from the boy who joins in the fever of excitement when the mackerel shoal inshore, to the experienced angler who waits over the deeps for shark; and the motivation is the desire to catch fish.

Perhaps the most important feature of angling is that it is a matter of personal interpretation. While traditionally cut-and-dried methods do undoubtedly yield fish, there is much scope for initiative, particularly in coping with conditions which vary from coast to coast. One cannot say *exactly* how and what will catch a particular species of fish, or even, for certain, where the fish are to be found. There may be local concentrations or anuual runs of big fish, or small fish, moving over shingle flats in relatively quiet water, or found in weed-strewn roughs, and one species alone could require any one of a dozen different methods according to locale. And so the writer can merely generalise, and perhaps offer a form of compromise from which the reader must make his own adaptations to suit whatever circumstances and conditions he encounters.

This book is not a complete guide to sea angling, for such is hardly within the grasp of one man to write, and, besides, there is still much to be learned about fish. Rather is it a book which portrays one man's angle on sea angling. In part, it may appear to the veteran to be almost naïve, to be aimed too much at the tyro, while to the tyro it may appear, at times, to be ultra-technical. Whatever the view, it is intended as a book from which both fraternities can learn, and the tyro, once the basics have been mastered, can refer to it time after time as he progresses in the sport.

And sea angling is a sport—make no mistake about that! The degree of sport which it affords is decided solely by the individual, by how he fishes and what he derives from his fishing, and if there is any success in angling it is in terms of catching fish.

That is what this book is about.

CHAPTER ONE

Tackle and Technique

RODS

THERE are many different designs of fishing rods currently
available for sea angling but, within limits, none so tremendously progressive as to show any real improvement
upon what is traditionally accepted as a rod. Many refinements
have been introduced as designers have considered the problems inherent in certain aspects, as in beach casting for instance,
but there can be only so much change in what, after all, is a very
simple tool. The *real* change has come about in materials, and
this change has been very marked as synthetic materials for rodmaking have been developed and perfected.

This section is but a broad introduction, more concerned with
the materials from which rods are made and the fittings which
go to make up a rod than with attempting to tell the reader
about a particular type of rod. What starts here expands to
greater detail as one gets further into the book and becomes involved with the different aspects of sea angling, which is when
the requirement for a particular type of rod becomes apparent.

Regardless of the type or nature of fishing anticipated, the
best flexing action one could possibly obtain in a rod, both in
casting and playing, would be in a rod constructed from one
continuous length of material. Obviously, with the exception
of very short boat rods, this is generally impractical, and ferrules
have to be incorporated so that the rod can be packed up for
travelling and general convenience. Unfortunately, ferrules tend

to break up the action when the rod is under stress, each ferrule providing a rigid, 'dead' point on the rod. Anglers with immediate access to fishing *do* have rods made up of one continuous length, but these are home-made or by special order, and the rods manufactured by the fishing-tackle industry are normally of two sections, joined midway by a ferrule. Many years ago, sea rods made up in three sections were commonly encountered, but today, to my knowledge, none of the leading rod-makers produces such rods.

The easiest rod to obtain or make in one continuous length is a short boat rod and the power from tip to rubber button in such a rod will enable one to beat a big fish relatively quicker

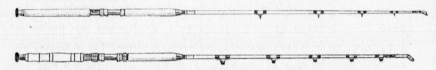

Conventional boat rods for light fishing and heavy duty

than with the conventional 'jointed' rod. Some boat rods are designed to give the maximum possible action, despite the ferrule; these have the ferrule at the top of the butt or under the reel fitting, leaving the rod length proper unhindered, with some of the action still imparted to the butt.

Choice of materials today rests normally with either solid or tubular fibreglass. Built-cane or split-cane rods—made up of sections split from Tonkin cane—can still be obtained, and there are anglers who will use no other material. But commercially produced cane sea rods are now few and far between. Built-cane is heavier than tubular glass, and does have to be cared for, but other than that, there is nothing wrong with cane as a rod-making material. The main snags are that good Tonkin cane is difficult to obtain, and craftsmen capable of making good cane rods are even harder to find. In the author's experience, there has never been a case of good built-cane breaking through any fault in the material itself; any breakages have been the result of poor, incorrectly treated cane, poor construction, or carelessness in allowing salt water to penetrate the cane. Some of the finest cane available at the present time comes from Clifford Constable, the Bromley rod-maker.

Glass fibre is extremely durable and, even with considerable abuse, able to stand up to the rigours of everyday fishing. Not so very long ago it was thought that only solid glass was suitable for deep-water rods, on the grounds that solid glass was less likely to shatter under stress than tubular glass, but this is not true. Strength in such materials should be thought of purely in terms of fishing, not abuse. Obviously, as tubular glass is made up of a thin wall of glass, it will not stand up to being trodden upon, or shut in car doors, but if one disregards negligence, then, in terms of fishing, tubular glass is superior to solid glass.

I always remember Dick Walker's pithy comment, on being told of the superiority of glass over built-cane and that with this material one could run into walls, drop it on a hard surface, or even chop down nettles with it. Dick agreed that for such purposes a glass-fibre rod might be excellent, but added that he used fishing rods for fishing, and for fishing he preferred built-cane.

Anglers might well think along these lines where solid and tubular glass is concerned. The fact that a solid-glass rod will stand up to being knocked about in a boat, while a tubular-glass rod may not, does not mean that a solid-glass rod is stronger than its tubular counterpart when flexed against a fish. In fact, with the emphasis nowadays on a graduated taper in the wall of a tubular rod, the action can be calculated and controlled. A solid rod tends to have a soft, floppy action, to lack the tension of tubular glass, and is comparatively heavy. The main advantages in favour of solid glass are tremendous durability and relative cheapness.

Some people tend to think that a fishing rod can be used as

a general-purpose rod, and do not realise that a rod can be overloaded, or underloaded. A particular rod will react as near perfectly as possible with a given breaking strain of line and weight of terminal tackle, but the further one deviates from this ideal loading, the poorer the tackle performance. There is, of course, a reasonable degree of tolerance either side, depending upon the rod, and one might go to extremes before realising that handling and casting quality had deteriorated. An idea of the best breaking strain of line to be used with a particular rod is afforded by a calculation based upon the *test curve* of that rod.

The test curve of a rod is the pull, measured on a spring balance, required to take the rod over into an arc of even curvature with the tip at right angles to the butt. Having read off the weight of pull to obtain the necessary curvature, one multiples this by five to reach a figure for the breaking strain of line to suit the rod. This figure provides a nucleus upon which to base the breaking strain of line, and a latitude of approximately 25 per cent either way can be allowed.

For example, a rod with a test curve of $2\frac{1}{2}$lb has a line breaking strain nucleus of $12\frac{1}{2}$lb. This could be stepped up to 16lb, or brought down to 9lb, with the rod handling any breaking strains of lines between these two figures.

Some beach-casting rods are specially designed to cast specified weights, and the weight involved will then decide the breaking strain of line to be used. As a rough guide, rods specified for

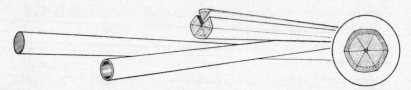

Solid glass, tubular glass, and built-cane rod blanks. The built-cane blank shows how sections are made up, and the inset indicates the tough outer skin area of the cane

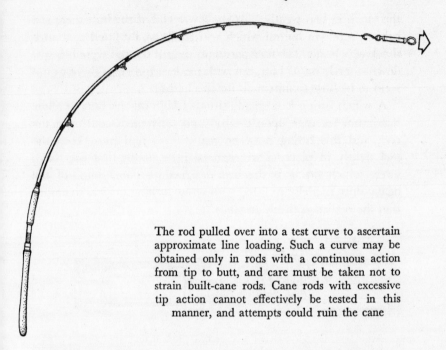

The rod pulled over into a test curve to ascertain approximate line loading. Such a curve may be obtained only in rods with a continuous action from tip to butt, and care must be taken not to strain built-cane rods. Cane rods with excessive tip action cannot effectively be tested in this manner, and attempts could ruin the cane

casting weights of between 2 and 4oz should carry lines of between 12 and 18lb breaking strain. Between 4 and 6oz lines between 18 and 24lb, and 6 and 8oz, between 24 and 30lb.

PARTS AND FITTINGS

Whatever the rod material, once this material is made up into lengths for fishing rods, the lengths are then known as 'blanks'. For example, strips of Tonkin cane glued together in a hexagonal length prior to finishing make up a built-cane blank, and a tapering length of glass fibre is a glass blank.

The handle of the rod is known as the 'butt', normally made up of cork rings or wood, and while cork is invariably the more expensive it does have advantages. It affords a good grip even when wet and, unlike wood, does not feel excessively cold to the touch in bad weather. At the lower end of the butt there is a rubber, screw-in button which was traditionally fitted to absorb shock which might shatter porcelain rings if the rod were brought down smartly on its butt, but with modern rod rings there would seem to be little requirement for this button.

A winch fitting is normally situated high on the butt to allow maximum leverage upon the rod and convenient control of the reel, and this fitting must be really firm, and must keep the reel tightly in place. There can be little doubt that the fixed, screw winch fitting is the best designed to date. Some of the heavy-duty models are fitted with screw locking devices to ensure that the reel stays firmly in place.

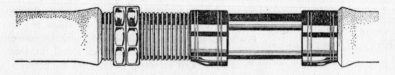

A conventional screw winch fitting

At one time, rings for sea rods were identified mainly by their bulky construction and linings of porcelain. While an old rod may still provide many years of usage, porcelain rings inevitably become cracked and chipped, despite care, and can ruin a line immediately afterwards. Today, rod rings tend to be less bulky, better designed, made of hard chromed steel, stainless steel or tungsten carbide and, when lined, fitted with linings made of synthetic materials which seem virtually indestructible.

On the heavy-duty boat rods used for the larger species, a roller end guide is fitted at the tip, and sometimes roller rings are fitted throughout. Unless one is to specialise in shark fishing, or large, fast fish such as swordfish, there is little call for roller rings in conventional boat fishing in European waters, and the cost of these rings is very high at present. However, a roller end guide can make light work of some aspects of deep-water fishing, and is an essential when metal lines are to be used.

Ferrules are normally constructed of brass, coated to prevent corrosion and reinforced to prevent damage to the walls. On some rods the ferrules may appear rather bulky, but this is a good point, for they should fit around the blank, as opposed to the blank being shaved down to fit the ferrule. One must watch out for this particularly in built-cane rods, for all the strength in cane is in the tough outer 'skin'. If this is shaved off to take a ferrule, then power is lost at a vital point.

While it is essential to keep ferrules clean and free of corrosion, some lubricants can attract dirt and grit. Trouble is seldom encountered if a ferrule-stopper is kept plugged in the female ferrule when the rod is not in use.

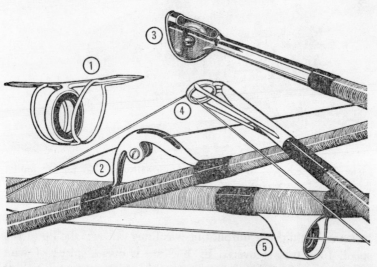

Various rod rings and guides. (1) Agatine lined, of a design normally used for spinning rods. (2) Aftco intermediate roller guide; normally used in big game or shark rods. (3) Single roller end guide; fitted to heavy-duty rods, or where metal line is to be employed. (4) Conventional end ring; made of tungsten carbide or stainless steel. (5) Agatine lined, tunnel ring; fitted to heavy-duty skate or shark rods

THE FIXED-SPOOL REEL

In 1905, Alfred Holden Illingworth invented the reel which is known today as the fixed-spool reel. With the axis parallel to the rod and the face of the spool at right angles to it, this reel was something of an enigma. Unlike the conventional rotating

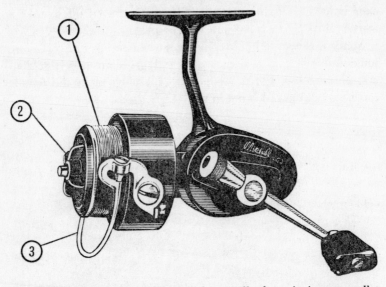

Light fixed-spool reel of a type used normally for spinning, or mullet fishing. (1) The spool, filled to capacity. (2) The slipping clutch. (3) Bail arm

reel, the line did not unroll, but was flung off over the lip of the spool. Line was recovered by hooking it over a piece of wire which laid it back upon the spool. Twenty years ago, fixed-spool reels were still relatively uncommon, very expensive, and few people understood fully how to use them. Today, despite mass production, lower prices, and a general acceptance of it, this reel is still something of an enigma to many anglers.

Casting with the fixed-spool reel is very easy, and it is this which makes it so very attractive. However, many anglers are content to load the spool with a comparatively heavy line and make cast after cast to take fish which are far below the weight required even to test these lines, and there, for them, the matter ends. It is only when a fish sufficiently large to need more than mere brute force and ignorance comes along that some of these anglers begin to realise that something is missing. Some blame their tackle when the inevitable breakages occur, but often the blame rests with the angler himself, for it is a sad fact that the majority of fixed-spool users do not use this type of reel to its full potential.

One should start off by understanding that anything which can be done with any other design of reel can be done with the fixed spool. When a fish is being played, the pressure on the fish is via the slipping clutch on the front of the spool. This clutch is incorporated in the reel as a kind of 'safety valve' to prevent the fish from breaking the line, and may be adjusted according to requirements. To get the most from the reel, experienced anglers constantly adjust the tension during the fight, for if you wind against the fish to check its run instead of using the slipping clutch augmented by finger pressure where necessary, you will achieve nothing. If the clutch is screwed down hard, you will have no buffer between reel and fish, and with the fish going one way and you winding another way there must be a breakage. Because the slipping clutch system is quite separate from the winding mechanism, no amount of winding will stop a running fish. Only clutch-tension control will effect this.

To understand how one uses the fixed spool, try to imagine that you have come with me to spin for bass from a boat looking on to a rocky headland. I am using a supple rod and reel with the spool loaded right to the lip with 8lb breaking strain line. After tying in the end tackle, I hook on a spring balance, ask you to hold it, and then adjust the clutch until a 5lb pull takes out line with the rod flexed. Now I know that the slipping clutch will operate well before the quoted breaking strain of my line is reached. If I had been on my own, I would have set the clutch to slip when the rod was pulled into an arc with the tip roughly at right angles to the butt.

I make a cast, give the handle a half turn to close the bail arm, and begin to work the lure back on a fluttering, erratic course.

About twenty-five yards from the boat, the rod thumps over and I have a fish on. It turns for the rocks and the slipping clutch whirs as line runs out. Because it takes more energy to start the clutch slipping than it does to keep it slipping, I am not immediately bothered about putting pressure on the spool with my finger. But now the clutch is purring constantly, and so I drop my index finger on to the spool to apply additional, light tension.

The bass is running for the rocks, going strongly, but still I make no attempt to wind in line. I just keep tension on the spool which cannot stop the fish but is sufficient to keep the rod pulled over into an arc and provide a tiring drag on the fish. During all this time I keep my eyes out on the water to where I gauge the fish to be. There is no need to look down at the reel to ascertain whether or not line is going out, for a clicker at the back of the spool provides an audible signal telling me when and how fast line is going out.

Now the fish is close to the rocks, and *now* I start to put more pressure on the spool. The fish is still not stopped, but is having to work much harder against the pressure. At the last moment, I clamp my hand over the front of the reel and apply side strain to pull the fish off course from the danger mark. The fish comes round with the strain but keeps running, this time across out front. Because there is no direct pull away from the rod, I lower the tip and wind in what slack line has resulted from the fish's change of course. This is my first attempt at retrieving any line. Feeling the weight of the fish at the end of the line, I apply finger tension to the spool and lift the rod tip, but the fish is a big one and not tired yet. I take my finger off the spool quickly as the fish begins some typical lunges and the rod tip pulls over savagely, the slipping clutch giving line with a series of spasmodic buzzes. Without the slipping clutch, those fast lunges could have broken the line.

The bass goes off on another run, the finger goes back on to the spool—harder this time—and now the fish begins to slow. I clamp the reel again, lean back on the rod, feel the fish pulled towards me, drop the rod tip, and quickly wind in slack line. The fish starts another run and I stop winding immediately, putting the pressure back on the spool until the fish slows. Then the reel is clamped, the rod is lifted and lowered, and line recovered quickly. This is known as 'pumping'.

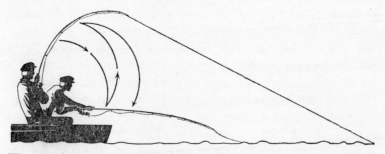

The pumping action. The rod tip is raised to draw the fish towards the boat, and then lowered quickly. Line is recovered only when the strain is off the rod

As I drag the bass towards the boat, you start to lower our big landing net, but the movement frightens the fish and it thrashes the water into foam in a series of mad dashes. Immediately, my finger comes off the spool and the slipping clutch buzzes several times—the second time the slipping clutch has saved my fish for me.

I put tension on the spool, start the fish coming towards the boat, and wind in line. Again the bass starts diving and lunging, but it is much weaker now and no longer has the strength to pull line against the clutch. Now I clamp the reel and get the fish over the net.

We have our first bass and, although it is a big one, you will have noticed that initially I made no attempt actually to pull the fish towards me, but rather let the fish tire itself by running against a light but insistent drag. At no time did I attempt to wind against the running fish, but recovered line only when I had been able to get slack line by pumping. In other words, you cannot use rod and reel simultaneously for recovering line. You must make line available with the power of the rod *first*, then get the rod tip down and use the reel to retrieve the slack line the rod has gained for you.

This emphasis upon the slipping clutch may suggest a somewhat involved routine, but once you come to terms with the reel you find clutch control coming automatically as the situation demands. You will discover that, with sufficient space and enough line, you can beat even the biggest fish. It is probable that you will be hesitant to yield your first big fish any line and, with clutch set tight, you will lose it. Then you will go to the other extreme, with hardly any tension, and lose your fish as it keeps running unimpeded, often into rocks or dense weed. This is a natural part of your apprenticeship with a fixed-spool reel, but it is an apprenticeship which is very well worth while, for the fixed spool is such a versatile piece of equipment that, once you have mastered it, you will find yourself able to fish in places and under conditions which would be virtually impossible with any other reel.

CASTING CONTROL

Now I make another cast at the rocks, but the weather has changed and a stiff crosswind is whipping up the sea. This time, I cannot make the casual cast that will drop the lure close to the rocks, but have to *punch* the tackle out to overcome the wind. I have to be careful now, for the wind can play havoc with fixed-spool casting unless one makes allowances for it.

This cast is a powerful one to ensure that I am accurate for direction, but the more I step up power the more difficult it becomes to maintain accuracy for range. Once the rod tip is pointing and the line is released and flowing from the reel, I extend my index finger alongside, but well clear of the edge of the spool. The line has to brush against my finger, and this brushing stops a great loop or belly of line from streaming out in the wind between rod tip and lure. The closer the lure gets to the target, the closer the finger comes in on the spool, and as each coil coming off the spool touches my approaching finger so the flow of line is restricted. As the lure comes into the target area—in this case, the bass rocks—I can bring my finger even closer to the edge of the spool and finally on to the lip itself. The gradually slowed lure drops into the water just where I want it, and, even more important, the belly of slack line is removed and the lure is immediately under control.

If I had neglected to use my finger to control the flow of line, the crosswind could have formed a great deal of slack, and while I was taking up this slack line the lure would have been out of contact and sinking, perhaps to become snagged in underwater rocks. With that strong, punching cast to beat the wind, I had to stop the lure from over-shooting, and if I had merely closed the bail arm I would have jerked the lure to a sudden stop in mid-flight, or even caused the lure and lead to part from the line. A sudden stoppage would have brought the lure springing back, with the same slack line and the same risk of loss.

POINTS TO CONSIDER

While there are some aspects of sea angling in which other types of reel perform better, a fixed-spool reel can be a decided asset for many methods. Certainly I would not be without a fixed-spool reel for my sea fishing, but it has to be the *right* fixed spool.. With so many models currently available to choose from, the angler contemplating the purchase of a reel for sea fishing should ensure that the model which pleases him at first glance is immune to saltwater corrosion—completely immune, that is!

For a reel should be truly proof against salt water, as opposed to 'resistant'—that much-loved word in the advertising world! To ensure proof against corrosion, metals like marine bronze and high-quality stainless steel have to be used to make even the smallest component part. And the prospective buyer should also ensure that claims for proofing extend to cover such easily forgotten items as holding screws and ball bearings, for salt penetrates even the closest-fitting casings to attack working parts. Thick paint will

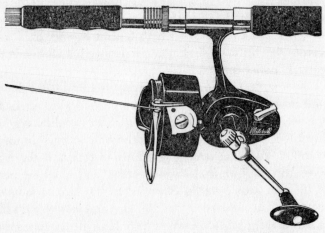

A large-capacity fixed-spool reel for beach and general shore fishing, in this instance, the Mitchell 386. This particular reel will carry 420yd of 15lb mono

cover well for a time, but when this chips, as eventually it must, the metal underneath must be intrinsically corrosion proof.

The weakest part of the fixed-spool reel is the bail arm. For ease and cheapness of manufacture, this is conventionally made up of several parts, and each joining link in the arm is a possible source of weakness at an already vulnerable point. Stipulate a reel with the bail arm made up of one piece of stainless steel. Such reels are widely available and will eliminate any risk of

connecting parts on an arm being loosened by the action of salt
water.

Incidentally, I have never yet met an angler who carried a
spare bail arm in his tackle box, though if that vital part were
to collapse on a Sunday morning on a remote storm-beach, then
fishing would probably be finished for the day.

THE MULTIPLYING REEL

The multiplying reel is often associated with American fishing,
and probably this is as it should be for in the United States the
multiplier is used in many more forms of angling than in Europe.
However, this reel started off in a very simple form in England,
was gradually lost to English use, and then returned in modified
form during the late 1920s, when it was so expensively priced
as to put it beyond the reach of all but a minority of anglers.
In the past, the only multiplying reels available in Britain were
imported from the USA and Scandinavia, but today these are
challenged by reels imported from France and, to some extent, by
British-made reels. While many imported items of fishing tackle
are of inferior quality to British-made products, it is only fair
to state that reels originating in the countries I have mentioned
are of the highest quality. In fact, the reels of Penn, ABU, and
Garcia are among the finest in the world. Conversely, I would
strongly advise against even considering the so-called multipliers
from Japan. The Japanese expertise, so well demonstrated in
cameras and some precision tools, does not extend to fishing
reels.

While the conventional centre-pin reel is of large diameter
and has direct drive, ie, one revolution of the drum for one turn
of the handles, the multiplier tends to be of small diameter with
the drive effected through gears to give several revolutions of the
drum for each turn of the handles. The number of revolutions
varies from model to model, but a ratio of around 3 to 1 is
general in good reels.

Though multiplying reels have traditionally been very wide across the drum, the modern trend is towards narrower drums, particularly for distance casting. This point is explained in detail in the section on Beach Casting.

Multipliers are basically much of a muchness, and to the casual glance the boat reel is merely a larger version of the beach-casting reel, but there are essential differences.

The multiplying reel is always used on top of the rod, and good models have non-slip rod clamps, the larger, very heavy models also having harness lugs to which a body harness may be attached. The handle, incorporating a star drag, is situated on the right of the reel, and this drag system allows the angler to control tension on the drum when the drum is engaged. The star drag can be thought of in much the same way as the slipping clutch on the fixed-spool reel. Used intelligently, it acts as a buffer between fish and angler, and decides whether one beats a big fish or suffers a breakage.

Some drags have indexed 'reminder' scales so that the reel can be re-set to any previous drag setting, and the best quality reels also have micro-fine adjustment to allow very accurate and precise brake settings ranging from 'right off' to 'full on'. Also on the right-hand side of the reel, above and to the rear of the handle seating, is the free-drum lever. This lever is pulled back to take the drum out of play, so that it runs freely without mechanical check—as in distance casting, or when lowering deep-water tackle rigs. Once the lever is in the rear position, control over the drum must be exercised by the thumb, although on some of the better quality reels there is a drum-tensioning device on the left-hand side of the reel. Make sure that this is not loosened so much that the drum moves from side to side, or there will be a risk of line tangling behind the drum flanges.

The 'freest' setting of all is when the drum can only just be rocked, barely perceptibly, from side to side. In this condition, the drum will not rattle in casting and there is no tension at all. A *slight* increase in tension may be beneficial to anglers at the stage when they are beginning to gain confidence in their casting, particularly when casting into a strong wind, when over-runs are most likely to occur. In boat fishing, this tension control is a definite asset, allowing adjustment to the reel to enable terminal tackle to drop speedily through the water, yet not so quickly that an over-run occurs when the lead touches bottom.

Some reels incorporate a level wind system, a wire loop which

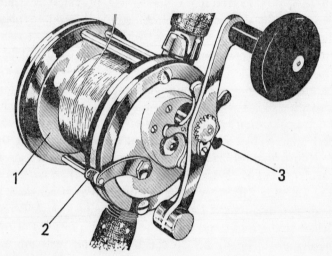

The Garcia 624 multiplier for boat fishing. (1) Bronze drum. (2) Drum release lever. (3) Indexed star drag

passes to and fro across the drum to distribute the line evenly, but one must remember that this system cannot be disengaged for casting, and a rapid side-to-side movement can only be to the detriment of casting.

As a boat reel, the ideal multiplying reel should be as large as weight and handling will allow, sturdy without sacrifice of precision, and have a large line capacity—at least 250yd of 30lb breaking-strain line. There must be great lifting power inherent in a boat reel and, of course, the drum should be strong. The best boat reels have drums made of bronze, designed to withstand the crushing pressures of all sizes of monofilament lines. All metal parts should be corrosion proof, and other parts should be as strong as modern materials will allow. With modern plastics, there is no longer any excuse for cracked or warped sideplates.

Boat fishing can be tiring, particularly in a long fight with a big fish, so, if you are contemplating buying a large-capacity boat reel and are confused by the various models available, there is an easy way to decide. A big handle provides tremendous leverage, a fair degree of comfort, and is a boon in playing a big fish, so look for the reel with the longest, balanced handle; preferably with a large handle knob which fills the palm.

As a shore-casting reel, the precision-made multiplier can be a joy to handle. Tools of the top casting men, these reels have to be precision-made if they are consistently to produce long, smooth casts. These reels do not need to be as sturdy as those intended for boat fishing and their design is more directed towards the achievement of distance in casting.

The essential difference is in the drum. For beach and pier casting, the drum must be as light as possible, yet still retain sufficient strength to stand up to the crushing pressures of nylon monofilament. The drums on the best casting reels are light-weights, made from reinforced plastics, but still guaranteed against breakages in the process of normal casting and fishing wear and tear. These reels are often accompanied by a spare drum, and this can be very important to shore fishing. The second drum can be ready-loaded with line of a different breaking strain, so that when changed conditions call for different tactics, one merely changes drums.

Fitting a spare drum to the casting reel is the only exception I make to my rule of not re-adjusting the drum tension nut on the left-hand end of the spindle. This is my own view, which I hold strongly, although one should always be guided by the maker's instructions—initially, anyway! If I am changing to a different breaking strain of line and different casting weight, then, natur-

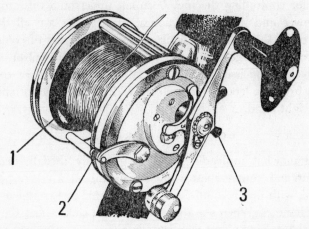

Garcia 602A Beachcaster. (1) Lightweight casting spool. (2) Drum release
lever. (3) Indexed star drag. This particular model, quite apart from
general fishing, has been used with great success in tournament casting

ally, I expect the drum to react differently when I make my
next cast. To counteract this, I adjust the tension nut until the
casting weight, with the rod held roughly at a 45-degree angle
from the ground, pulls the line easily and smoothly through the
rod rings under its own weight without coaxing. If the lead does
not fall easily, I ease off. If it falls in a rush, I tighten a fraction.
Once set, the nut stays set, for I believe one should come to terms
with the reel rather than tinker excessively in trying to get the
tension 'just right' for every cast. I rather like the idea of casting
without restriction of any sort, however slight, but until such
time as I have accustomed myself to the feel of different terminal
tackle, the drum tension provides a safety clause. As I have mentioned, this is purely a personal thing, and guidance should be
taken from reel instruction leaflets which are normally available
with good reels.

Condemnation for multipliers in some circles hinges about the
fact that the handle and star drag are on the right-hand side,
and most anglers are right-handed and like to use their 'good'

C

hand for controlling the rod. I cannot understand this attitude, for power and merely the vaguest directioning are all that is required of the rod hand, while sensitive exercising of control is required of the reel hand. To my mind, correct control of the reel decides the issue with a big fish in play, and best control comes from the 'good' hand which, with the majority of anglers, is the right hand.

CENTRE-PIN REELS

This somewhat misleading term is generally used to describe conventional 'round' reels which revolve about a centre pin, or spindle, with one revolution of the drum for one complete turn of the handles. When sea anglers talk about centre-pins, they are invariably talking about the virtually obsolete Nottingham reel— a comparatively small wooden reel with brass fittings; the Scarborough reel—an old-fashioned, wide-diameter reel still quite widely used on the north-east coast, or modern design large-capacity boat reels which are generally quite uncomplicated.

In my opinion, most of these reels are relics of the past, and have been superseded by the fixed-spool and the multiplying reel. The only exception to this is in boat fishing, where modern boat reels can be unbeatable if one is seeking a reel with a big capacity for lines of very high breaking strains. Such a reel will be laterally compressed, used beneath the rod, and will have little of the tiring, side-to-side wobble inherent in some large multiplying reels. Ideally, one should think in terms of a diameter of at least six inches, for there is no high-gear ratio to aid line recovery as in multiplying reels, and line recovery is related to the diameter of the reel. With such a simple design of reel, it can be very difficult work trying to beat a heavy fish in deep water, and that first wonderful feeling of direct contact with the fish can soon degenerate into one of sweated labour. If you are set on this type of reel for boat fishing—and this should preferably be for really heavy-duty work—then choose a model with large handles, and also with a lever-operated drag.

FISHING LINES

Coarse braided and twisted linen lines were at one time the hallmark of the sea angler, and seem to have remained in general use in sea angling long after coarse fishermen had been almost completely won over to synthetic materials. Now, everybody uses the synthetics. Nylon monofilament is undoubtedly most widely used, and for the widest range of purposes, from beach casting to deep-water boat fishing, but anglers are now becoming educated to the specialised benefits of braided nylon or terylene. In very recent years, metal line has also gathered disciples for deep-water boat fishing, but this is not a type of line to be treated casually.

Nylon monofilament is comparatively inexpensive, has slightly higher casting efficiency than braided nylon, offers less resistance to air and water currents, and is very durable, even without special care. Monofilament is approximately 25 per cent weaker than the quoted breaking strain when wet, tends to stretch considerably, and faults in the line are less likely to be noticed than those in braided lines. As the strength of monofilament is in its diameter, there may be unapparent weakness in a length which has been subjected to strain and thus had its diameter reduced. While nylon monofilament can be used for many aspects of sea angling, the elasticity of this type of line renders it unsuitable for really effective control of big fish in deep water.

Braided terylene is comparatively expensive, and available either as braided core or solid. The former has braiding about an inner line, the latter is solid line throughout. Either variety has considerably less tendency to stretch than nylon monofilament. Braided terylene shows faults in the obvious sign of fraying, and to be kept in good, supple condition, should be washed frequently in fresh water. The solid variety of braided terylene is ideal for deep-water fishing, for none of the power of the rod is lost through stretch in the line.

The life of a line can be extended if, after fishing, one makes a long cast, winds the line back through a folded piece of rag between the rod rings and distributes it evenly over the drum with the forefinger and thumb of the leading hand.

Monel metal line has been available for two or three years now, but has yet to achieve any wide degree of popularity. While it is a type of line which offers advantages to boat anglers, one has to understand the technique of using it.

The wire line comes into its own when the strength of the tide is such that weights in excess of 8oz are required to keep the bait near the bottom. In fact, wire line will enable the angler to fish tide races with approximately half the weight required by conventional lines to maintain position, and in some instances will allow fishing in Spring tides normally considered so strong as to be unfishable. There is no stretch in the wire line, and thus bite indication and control of a fish can be very positive.

The main disadvantage of the wire line is its tendency to kink, but this can be avoided if it is correctly handled. Tension must be kept on the line at all times; if you let the bait rush down on a free drum, on reaching the seabed the line will coil down on the bottom. Then, when line is recovered, it will be found to be kinked. The correct method is to keep control of the drum with the thumb during the descent, and to engage the drum the moment the lead is felt to hit the seabed. Use of wire line should be restricted to reels with metal drums, and rods with a roller guide at the tip. To my knowledge, metal line is available in three breaking strains: 20, 30, and 40lb.

HOOKS, LEADS, AND TERMINAL FITTINGS

When the average angler buys a rod or reel there is lengthy discussion and examination before a decision is arrived at. That rod, or reel, is handled time and time again until the angler is convinced it will do the things he expects of it. Besides which, it will also have to *look* right. Having equipped himself with the more substantial and expensive items of tackle, the average angler will then, almost as an afterthought, consider hooks. He may have a rough idea of the various sizes he will need, but that is probably as far as his concern will go.

The general tendency is to put all the emphasis upon such relatively expensive purchases as rods and reels, and to take the smaller, inexpensive items for granted. One can readily understand some hesitation in accepting the first rod or reel the salesman offers, for considerable money is involved, but it is difficult to understand why hooks, because they happen to be inexpensive items, should so often be treated casually. In terms of fishing, this is a peculiar sense of values.

If we really consider the facts of the matter, the rod and reel are refinements to catching fish, not essentials. The essentials of the game are the hook and line, the hook the all-important contact between fish and angler, and the line the means of maintaining that contact. The rod *is* important for placing that hook and line, and the reel for conveniently carrying and aiding control of the line, but when one comes to weigh it all up these are simply refinements leading to the most efficient methods of establishing contact with the fish. If the hook will not secure the fish, then contact is lost and the rest of the tackle is worthless.

Shortly after the second world war, when sea-angling tackle was somewhat limited in range and improvisation was the order of the day, anglers tended to think discerningly about such things as hooks. There were no fashionable rods as such, most of the tackle was pretty rough and ready, and though your rod might break or your reel jam, there was always the line to be taken in hand as the angler resorted to basic measures. Today, superlative rods and reels tend to divert one's mind away from the basics, yet, after all, this is still where the real issue lies.

The hook is possibly the cheapest single item of tackle but its vital importance bears no relation to its modest price. A pound saved on the price of a rod or reel to enable one to purchase better-quality hooks would be an investment indeed. The selection

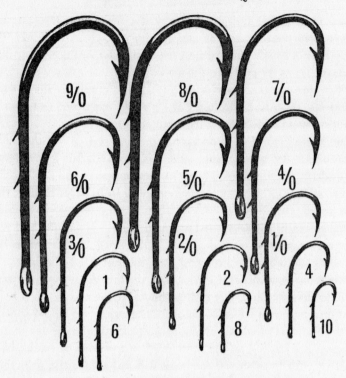

A range of Sealey Octopus hooks shown actual size

of hooks to be carried depends upon the type of fishing in which the angler plans to engage. For those setting out to embrace all forms of sea angling, many types and sizes of hooks will be required, from comparatively tiny, fine-wire models to seemingly huge, forged hooks.

The identification of hooks by size invariably causes confusion to the beginner, who will probably find little rhyme or reason in the system. For example, hooks may be numbered 1 to 8. In this case, the larger the identifying number, the smaller the size of the hook. Thus a size 8 hook is very small by comparison to a size 1, which is seven times bigger than the size 8. Once the identifying number is followed by /0, then the system becomes more logical. Now, the larger the identifying number, so the larger the size of the hook. Thus an 8/0 is approximately double the size of a 4/0.

Apart from size, there are different styles of hook for different species of fish, and, as extremes, there are fine-wire, long-shanked hooks for flounders in small sizes and shaped to accommodate worm baits, and forged steel, barbed shanks for bass or cod in medium sizes, barbed to hold a bait along the length of the hook and strongly made to stand up to big fish. Whatever the hook, it is attached to the line by an 'eye' or a 'spade end', but these terms do not identify the hook from the angler's point of view. What does help to describe the hook, are the design and length of the shank, or the shape in the bend of the hook. Consequently, a long-shank hook may have either an eye or a spade end at the top of the shank.

There tends to be accepted sizes of hooks for different species

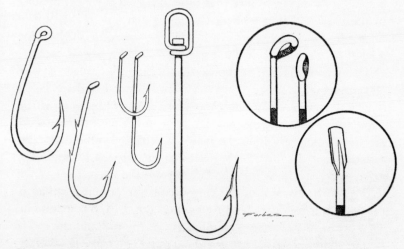

Various types and styles of hooks. From left to right: In-curve, barbed shank, short shank, long shank—invariably fine-gauge wire, swivelled conger hook. Insets show standard methods of attachment; eyed hooks—turned-down eye and straight eye, and spade end

of fish, but fish will show size variance within the species and it
is best to relate hook sizes to the bait to be used. While one could
give an acceptable size of hook for, say, flounders, and know that
the variation in the size of mouths of different-sized flounders
would be fairly negligible, one could not be so definite for bass.
There is no relating the difference in size of mouth of a 2lb
school bass to that of a 10 or 12lb bass. Likewise cod and tope.
For flounders, a size 2 long-shank hook could reasonably be
expected to account for all the flounders one contacts, while a
size 1/0 barbed-shank could be ideal for the average run of bass,
but inadequate for the occasional outsize fish.

As, within limits, one cannot tell the size of the species one
is likely to contact, the hook must be scaled to the size of bait,
for this also makes for balanced fishing. Very small hooks tend
to tear out of large baits in casting, and the point may become
muffled by the bait on the strike. While small and medium-size
hooks may afford a really first-class purchase in the mouth of a
big fish, one must consider that these smaller hooks will be finer
in the wire and thus will tend to straighten out to the pull of
a big fish. Over-large hooks may work loose and be shed during
a lengthy fight with a medium-size fish.

The larger the size of hook, the thicker the gauge of wire
and, invariably, the less sharp the point. When these large hooks
have to be used, a better purchase can be assured by working the
point with a whetstone or fine file prior to fishing, and by checking the point every time the tackle is retrieved. One must also
consider that the large hook has to be driven well home on the
strike to set the hook into the fish beyond the barb. Long-range
fishing, with any size of hook, also calls for powerful strikes if
the hook is to be set to hold throughout the fight, but unless one
is fishing with line related to the curve of the rod and the rod is
supple, sharp, powerful strikes at long range can cause breakages.

When buying hooks in the smaller sizes, do not hesitate to
test them by pulling the point away from the direction of the
shank. Good hooks will spring back into shape after pressure has

been applied, but beware of those which settle into the shape to which you have pulled them. For heavy-duty work, the finest hooks available are those made of forged stainless steel. These hooks will be fairly expensive, but they will stand up to salt-water corrosion much better than their bronzed counterparts. Also, avoid keeping your hooks collectively in a small tin—very much a popular habit with some sea anglers. This is just asking for dulled points, tangled masses which take time to sort out, and the spreading of rust and corrosion. Obtain a sectioned box in which to segregate hooks of different styles and sizes, even incorporating oil-soaked pads to protect the hooks. Try to avoid keeping rusted and corroded hooks. You may be tempted to use them at one time or another, and they could cost you fish.

The following is a very rough guide to hook sizes for different species:

Bass	1/0–3/0
Bream	4, 6. or 8
Cod	4/0–8/0
Conger	4/0–10/0
Common Skate	6/0–10/0
Thornback	3/0–5/0
Ling	4/0–6/0
Pollack	2/0–4/0
Tope	6/0–10/0
Whiting	1–4
Mullet	12–6 (Freshwater scale)
Wrasse	2, 4, or 6
Flounder	2–4
Plaice	1
Turbot	6–8

In the final analysis, the size and type of bait to be used, plus what size of fish the locale has to offer, will control hook sizes. However, until such time as the angler understands these factors fully, hook sizes within the limits shown for the various species will act as a guide, but only as a guide. If it is found that a size outside the limits for a certain fish produces fish consistently, taking into consideration bait and fish-holding qualities, then, obviously, that is the hook for the job.

WEIGHTS

There are many varying designs of sea-fishing weights, but on a general basis they can be divided into two groups, the casting leads, shaped to perform well in flight, and the holding leads, designed to hold bottom. Between the two groups are various designs of leads which attempt to offer a compromise.

In this section I shall merely illustrate the various lead designs and refrain from detail. The pros and cons of different designs of leads is fully covered in the Beach Casting and Boat Fishing sections, and, where applicable, in the descriptions of other fishing techniques.

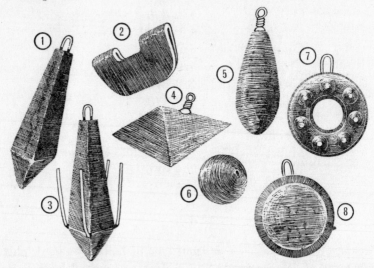

A selection of conventional leads. (1) Torpedo or pyramid. (2) Fold-over lead, generally used for spinning. (3) Spiked torpedo. (4) Capta. (5) Pear or bomb. (6) Drilled bullet. (7) Grip lead. (8) Watch lead

My own feeling is that one could well dispense with many of the popular designs—the Jardine spiral and grip leads are abominations!—and enjoy all-round fishing with aerodynamically efficient leads for beach casting, and pear and Capta leads for deep-water work. Drilled bullets, sheet lead, and split shot would complete the outfit and allow one to cope with most normal situations. Spiked torpedo leads give a good grip on the seabed, but often sap the power in the strike, for the manufactured leads invariably have spikes which are too long. One can alleviate the problem somewhat by snipping off part of the spikes to suit conditions.

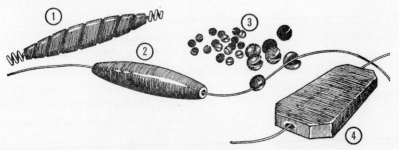

(1) Jardine spiral. (2) Barrel lead. (3) Split-shot: in the largest size known as swan shot, in the smallest size, dust shot. (4) Coffin lead

Whatever design of weight you choose, let prevailing conditions dictate the actual weight of lead, and aim to use as light a weight as conditions will allow. Bear in mind, too, that, in beach casting, weight will be governed to a great extent by the rod and breaking strain of line you are to use.

SWIVELS

Swivels are designed for specific purposes, but the main function is to prevent twist being imparted to terminal tackle or main reel line, with consequent weakening somewhere between the hook and the reel. Quite apart from reducing the risk of line-twist to a minimum, swivels allow one to design terminal rigs with ingenuity, and safety, and to change rigs, or part of the rig, speedily and efficiently.

Swivels are fairly intricate and faults may be inherent in the method of manufacture. As swivels are also relatively expensive, one should feel no embarrassment whatsoever on checking each swivel individually and ensuring that all are sound before leaving a tackle shop.

There can be considerable strength in a swivel, so do not over-load terminal tackle for the smaller species with outsize swivels. Conversely, ensure that the swivels incorporated in tope or conger rigs are proportionate to the strength of the trace. When assembling spinning rigs, lead attached direct to the line should always come between the last swivel and the rod top. Finally, always check your swivels for corrosion between fishing trips and endeavour to keep them well oiled.

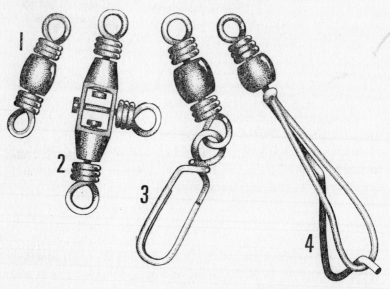

A selection of commonly used swivels. (1) Barrel swivel. (2) Three-way swivel. (3) Link swivel. (4) Swivelled buckle

TRACES

Traces for conventional fishing are very much a matter of personal ingenuity, best kept as simple as possible, and one soon finds that simplicity can be difficult.

Obviously, traces for spinning and beach casting need to be

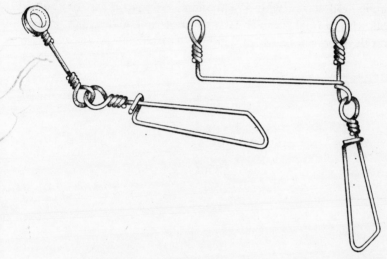

(1) Kilmore running boom. (2) Clements boom

as streamlined as possible, with no unnecessary fittings to set up air resistance. Complicated set-ups invariably result in a tangled heap on the seabed, or in the boat, and this contributes nothing to fishing efficiency. Try to get away with as little as possible and with as few knots as possible in your trace, and where booms are necessary, the Clements or Kilmore boom should suit most situations.

My own practice is to make up traces in my spare time, literally dozens of them, each planned for a different purpose at some future date. If one works on this basis, knots and lengths of nylon for traces can be checked at leisure and far more thoroughly than would be possible in the course of normal fishing.

Be particularly careful when working with wire traces for the larger species, and ensure that strength conforms between swivels and connections. Check old, plastic-covered wire traces for nicks in the plastic covering which may have allowed corrosion to set in. Bear in mind, too, that every knot and every swivel in a trace is a potential source of weakness, and where possible, tie simple knots and secure with a whipping. Whippings can be finished off with normal commercial varnish if time allows, but, if done on the spot, can be sealed with nail varnish.

CHAPTER TWO

Baits and Lures

THE baits and lures which we present to fish should represent food in some form. At one time, I would have written *natural* food, but the instances of sea fishes taking the most weird and wonderful things—consider the plastic cups found so commonly nowadays inside cod!—are so frequent that I am now prompted to believe that one merely has to offer a suggestion of food, rather than a natural replica of some food form. The perfect bait, viewed by a fish, looks as though it *could* be eaten, and moves as though it *should* be eaten.

Regardless of the lure or bait involved, the main deterrent to its success might be not that it looks unnatural, but rather that it is presented on tackle which makes it react unnaturally in the water. Within limits, rather than worry overmuch about the type of bait, it would seem better to concentrate on how to present that bait. While an angler can throw out a lure, retrieve it as fast as possible, and in the process hook a large bass, he will not do it consistently. And successful fishing is consistency, not the infrequent catching of fish by chance. To catch fish consistently, you have to rely upon calculated methods and technique, not chance.

Marine worms, if the bait-digging industry is anything to go by, is the most popular bait of the average angler, and while these worms can be very effective for many forms of fishing, the sea angler who restricts himself solely to worms will find—like the coarse fisherman who limits himself to maggots—that a lot of sport is being missed. However, the effectiveness of a bait is

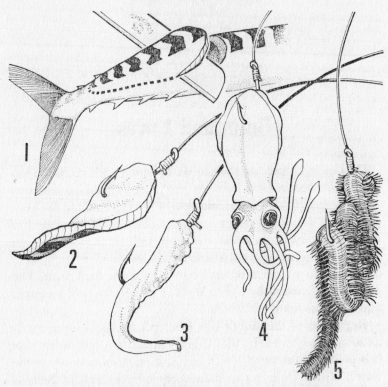

Some baits which are widely used to good effect in sea angling: (1) Last being cut from tail section of mackerel. (2) Mackerel last on hook. (3) Squid tentacle. (4) Immature squid. (5) Ragworm, bunched to withstand shock of casting

best shown by the number and quality of fish it yields, and where conditions and locale lend themselves to fishing worm, then worm can be unbeatable. The main snag with worms as a bait is their availability, for anglers tend to accept them as the only bait and consequently, when they are not available, feel that nothing else will catch fish. That may sound rather strange, but it is a peculiar fact that anglers fish better and more successfully with baits and tackle in which they have confidence.

Watch an angler spinning who has never caught a fish by

spinning before. It is a fairly safe bet that he is uncertain, doubtful of the wisdom of winding a piece of metal through the water,
and if there is no result he will return to normal bait fishing
almost with relief. Still there may be no result, but he knows
that the method has taken fish for him before, and will again.
But watch what happens if a fish pulls the rod over in the initial
stages of spinning. Then our angler becomes a picture of concentration, prepared to work that lure for the rest of the day,
now that he knows it can be used to good effect.

It is failure to try a new technique or bait for fear of wasting
valuable fishing time which spoils the chances of catching more
or bigger fish for so many anglers.

Lugworm and ragworm are the two bait forms known to all
sea anglers. Both are dug from the shore below the tide line,
and the best specimens come from stretches made up of a mixture
of mud and shingle. There are several varieties of ragworm, most
of which are very small, but the one of most interest to anglers
is known as king rag, a variety which sometimes exceeds 12 inches
in length. These worms really come into their own when fished
over mud and shingle banks, particularly for flatfish, but they
must be in good condition. Unfortunately, they are apt to die

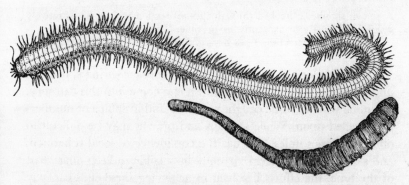

This fringed marine worm, the ragworm, is the basic bait of the average
sea angler. Less easily obtained, and requiring considerable care when
mounting on the hook, the lugworm also has its share of devotees. It is
essential that hooks be needle-sharp to present these baits to best advantage

D

extremely quickly, become soggy, or dry out, and are then virtually impossible to cast intact and unattractive as bait. Various methods, some quite complicated and ingenious, are quoted for keeping them in good condition, but the best known to the author is to wrap the worms individually in newspaper and store them in a cool, dark place.

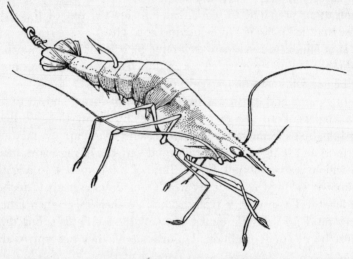

A prawn should be hooked through the tail section with a comparatively small hook and cast as gently as possible. This crustacean can prove a superb bait when fished just beyond surf, or close to rock outcrops

Live baits, for all practical purposes, embrace shrimps, prawns, and sand-eels. Many other small fish can come into this category, but none which can be caught regularly and in sufficient numbers to be relied upon. While shrimps and prawns may be difficult to obtain at times unless one has the confidence of local fishermen, and sand-eels might seem virtually impossible to keep alive most of the time, the efforts involved in achieving these ends can pay dividends.

Sand-eels are normally netted with a fine-mesh seine, but the casual angler in the right locale can dig along the low-water

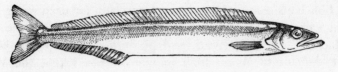

Sand-eel

mark for them with a fork. A special hook-type implement is
traditionally used for scraping in the sand for these creatures as
a spade tends to damage them, but one can get by with the conventional garden fork. Sand-eels can burrow very quickly once
disturbed and many will be missed, but there is consolation in
the fact that where sand-eels are to be found, they are usually
to be found in large numbers.

Sand-eels are normally kept alive in a *courge*—a container
made of wicker-work, which is towed behind a boat on the way
out to a mark. They will not live long in a bucket or other metal
container, even though the water be changed constantly. For
practical purposes, a fine-mesh keepnet can retain the sand-eels
in fairly good condition, but they should not be handled un-
necessarily. When intended live-baits cannot be kept alive, they
can still be used to good effect, particularly when fished just
beyond the surf.

Lengthy fish cutting can be kept well up over the hook by whipping a
tiny hook to the trace to take the weight of the bait. This advantage,
alternatively, may be gained by fixing a swan shot to the trace and tying
the end of the bait over this shot

Fish baits come into their own especially for deep-water use, but various fish can be utilised in cuttings and fillets inshore. Mackerel, herrings, sprats, and pilchards—although the latter are difficult to obtain fresh in many areas, except the West Country—are all very oily fish which make first-class baits. Lengthy fillets from the flanks of such fish will show up nicely, even in coloured water, and the traditional mackerel 'last', or

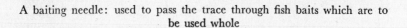

A baiting needle: used to pass the trace through fish baits which are to be used whole

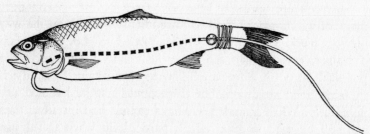

The setting-up of whole fish as baits is much a matter of personal ingenuity, but trace attachments to swivels, etc, must be made after the fish has been mounted to ensure clean line passage through the fish. In this instance, the bait has been tied by the tail and a swan shot added to the trace to prevent the hook from pulling up through the soft underside

'lask', cut from the toughest part of the mackerel, can be very durable, even in fast water. Sprats and small pout can often be used whole, mounted with a baiting needle, and whole mackerel and herrings in fresh condition make good tope baits.

Shellfish in various forms can be used successfully, but I do not share the enthusiasm of some anglers for this bait form, regarding it as acceptable only when nothing else is available, and then not enjoying the problems of keeping it on the hook. Mussels, cockles, and such baits can be toughened by boiling, and will then stay on the hook well. Unfortunately, the boiled product loses the attraction it has for fish in the natural state.

Crabs *can* be good bait, but I restrict their use to boat fishing for bottom-dwelling fish, and then, like shellfish, only when other bait is difficult to obtain. Much is made by some experienced anglers about 'peeler' or 'shedder' crabs—a stage of crab growth after the hard shell has been shed, and the new, pliable shell is in the process of hardening—but if large fish are to take crabs, then, in my experience, they are not unduly bothered about the shells being hard. I normally kill the crab, remove the claws to reduce the risk of small fish tugging to give false bite indication, break the shell carefully and then wind a stout rubber band about it. The hook is passed under and through the rubber binding, not through the shell.

Squid and cuttle cuttings make superb baits which stay on the hook well, particularly if a binding is used to keep the flesh well up on the hook in fast water. In many delicatessen stores it is possible to buy tiny squid by the pound, and these, used whole, are some of the best baits obtainable, either for boat fishing or inshore for large bass.

Spoons, spinners, and bars can be tremendous lures for mackerel, bass and pollack, but it is a sad fact that lures have a special sort of magnetism which attracts more anglers than fish. I shall never forget the rather elderly angler on a groin near Plymouth some years ago. He was spinning, without much success, and eventually we got to talking. He delved into his tackle box and produced a small canvas bag from which he carefully withdrew a small lure. 'This', he said, with obvious pride of possession, 'is the very famous Mevagissey sand-eel'. He went on to tell me of the wonderful reputation his lure had for taking fish, but the poor man wouldn't use it for fear of losing it.

Not all anglers are like that, of course, but the majority do tend to pick lures which please them for aesthetic reasons, pay lots of money in the process, and do not consider how fish will react to them. Much of the beautiful colour treatment in lures

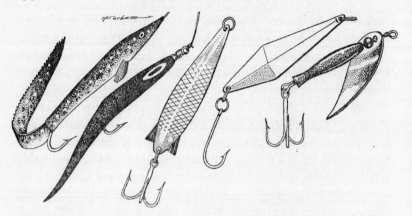

Lures which can be used inshore to good effect, particularly with bass and pollack: Two variations on a rubber sand-eel. Toby lure. ABU Prisma—in its smallest size and, in this instance, with single hook replacing treble. Vibro or Gillarex spoon

is lost on fish, and quite possibly colour in itself is relatively unimportant, beyond the fish-like silvers and bronzes. What *is* important is the shape of the lure and the way that lure moves in the water.

Having settled for a lure which you feel will act in the water like a small, abstract fish—and after all, lures are supposed to represent small fish—the secret behind successful spinning is to work the rod and reel to impart 'life' to the lure, retrieving as slowly as you possibly can, so that the movement potential of the lure is exploited to the full. A general fault in spinning is a desire to cast the lure as far as possible and then retrieve it in the fastest possible time. Even with fast-retrieve reels, it is improbable that one could retrieve fast enough to beat a bass, mackerel, or pollack which is streaking after the lure, but most fish tend to ignore a fast, constant movement. Far better to disregard distance, to pick out a particular area and concentrate on that area, relying on short, accurate casts, retrieving through gullies and around rocks and pilings with the lure wobbling and jerking on a slow, erratic course.

Predatory fish can sometimes be seen to follow a lure time after time, lose interest, and then turn away. When this happens, the angler needs to start thinking about varying the rate of retrieve, or, if that seems in order, changing lures.

Where spinning is concerned, it is not what you have, but what you do with it that counts. Where general angling is concerned, an open mind will pay dividends. Do not worry about a traditional bass rig, or a standard cod rig. Weigh up the situation and the prevailing conditions, and make up a rig to suit those conditions. Ingenuity will often produce fish when standard methods fail.

Persistent spinning through one area may prompt well-fed bass to strike purely through aggression

CHAPTER THREE

Beach Casting

TWENTY years ago, it would have seemed highly improbable that an average angler could have cast a lead over one hundred yards from the beach into the sea. Indeed, it is doubtful if there were a score of anglers capable of such a feat. Today the scene has changed. Today, there is specialised beach-casting tackle designed to overcome the problems of long-distance casting, and materials have changed, too.

In casting rods, tubular glass fibre has replaced green-heart and built-cane, and precision reels have made the old wooden centre-pins virtually obsolete. And, perhaps even more important, a trend has developed towards greater discernment in fishing.

Fishing from the shore is no longer the less refined cousin to other forms of angling. It has become popular, almost fashionable, for several factors inland have contributed towards a great swing to the sea for sportfishing, and change came with the growth of popularity. Men of some discernment replaced the traditionalists—the men who fished as their fathers, and *their* fathers before them, had fished—and the newcomers sought solutions for angling problems, promoted the finer points and revolutionised tackle and techniques.

Among the new-wave anglers, a giant of a man named Leslie Moncrieff began to gather disciples to his methods and achieved angling fame in a revolution which was to educate anglers—and the fishing tackle industry—as to the tackle necessary for long-distance beach casting, and the fishing potential in such casting.

There are, and have been, greater casting champions than

Moncrieff, but none has influenced a form of angling so greatly. Now, beach anglers tend to be more conscious of their casting ability and practise to achieve greater distances; and the majority of beaches make long-distance casting essential for consistently successful angling.

To appreciate the benefits which come from distance casting, one should envisage a popular venue with, shall we say, *average* anglers spaced out at 20yd intervals. The fish have been coming in well, the angling press has been quick to herald the fact, and consequently anglers have come from far and near to fish the tide. These anglers are making distances of between 60 and 80yd in their casts, each throwing out his own particular permutation of tackle. Casting leads probably range from two to eight ounces in weight, the lines are festooned with all manner of booms and paternosters and—as is often the way with anglers— the fewer bites, the more frequent the casting becomes.

Now consider the seabed some 70yd from that beach. Leads continuously smash down into the water until the area must seem a veritable firing range. It is true that the descent of one lead must seem a mere ripple in a very large ocean, but it is also true that fish are ultra-sensitive to sharp, unusual vibrations in their turbulent but constant environment. Concentrate the vibrations from many leads falling into a restricted area and it is conceivable that the fish will move out of that area. This, of course, is speculation—as it must be when one attempts to define reaction in another element's creatures—but success often depends upon the accuracy of one's speculations. But, whichever way you look at it, it is reasonable to believe that fish can be driven further out by excessive disturbance, in which case the angler who is able to extend his casting by twenty or thirty yards will probably find the fish.

Envisage another situation, this time a deserted beach and only the forces of nature to contend with. The sea has worked a deep gulley out of the shingle, and into this gulley the current has drawn sufficient natural food to make the depression attractive to fish. An angler casts streamlined tackle from the beach, again and again, but does not reach the gulley where the fish are concentrated. Then he gets the feel of his tackle, makes the extra distance, and drops his bait among the fish in the gulley. True, our imaginary angler would need knowledge of such a mark, but knowledge here would be wasted without the ability to make use of it.

The most dramatic example of such a situation is to be found along the Kent coast, at Dungeness, for there the sea sweeps ton upon ton of shingle against Dungeness Point, and as the fast water moves around this point towards Dymchurch Bay it swings back off the shingle to create a giant eddy. This eddy is very deep, almost 100yd from the beach, and is known to anglers as 'The Dustbin'. To put the bait into the 'Dustbin' at full tide needs a cast of 120yd; at low tide, a cast of 80yd.

Those who can make the distance at Dungeness frequently catch cod, those who cannot invariably remain fishless. It was at Dungeness, with its now-famous gulley, that Moncrieff proved time and time again the effectiveness of long-distance casting.

It is true to say that it is not always necessary to cast great distances to catch fish, for sometimes the sea promotes conditions which concentrate natural food close inshore and fish are attracted to it. However, the ability to cast a long distance is an almost essential qualification for the beach angler and may well decide the issue of whether he catches fish or not.

BEACH-CASTING TACKLE

Modern beach-casting rods are made of tubular glass fibre. No other material offers the advantages inherent in glass fibre; its lightness for length, its durable properties—important where salt water is concerned—and its power. A well-designed glass rod is a joy to cast with and, while there must always be compromise between a good casting tool and an efficient fishing rod, it is capable of handling the heaviest fish the beach angler is likely to encounter.

The generally accepted standard length of rod for beach casting is 12ft, but, while many sections of the fishing-tackle industry insist on producing only 12ft rods, the most efficient length of rod must inevitably be dictated by the physique and capabilities of the angler.

While velocity at the point of releasing the lead is governed by the arc covered by the rod tip—from which one deduces that the longer the rod the greater the arc, the higher the velocity, and consequently the further the cast—the angler must fit the rod to himself rather than try to come to terms with a stipulated 'necessary' length. The correct length is the length one is able to wield with maximum effect.

A 6ft angler using a 12ft 6in rod may find his casts being equalled by an angler only 5ft tall using a 10ft rod but otherwise identical tackle. Height of the angler, as opposed to strength, seems to be the determining factor for the length of rod. Technique, much more than strength, is what makes for good casting, and the short man may find an extra-long rod just that little bit too awkward to enable him to concentrate fully on his casting action. Conversely, the tall man may find that he has not been able to generate full power into his cast by the time the tip of an unduly short rod has travelled to the point where the lead should be released.

Actual design of the rod depends upon the theories and fancy of the individual but, unfortunately, one can never be sure, at the beginning, which design will suit, and there is no really practical way of finding out before one buys a rod.

There has been much controversy in the angling press in recent years between various schools of casting thought, with one offering a most convincing argument one week, only to have it demolished with equal conviction the following week by another school. Each school of thought seems to produce casters capable of casting very impressive distances. Some favour the 'Spring-heel', or

'Spring-butt', a rod with the butt constructed from a blank with a reverse taper in its wall, designed to act like a long bow, the theory being that the extra movement in the tapering butt provides more power and reduces jerking action, thus enabling a greater variety of casting weights to be used without fear of the line parting. Reduction of the jerking action also reduces over-rapid spool acceleration and risk of over-runs.

Opposite reverse-tapered rods are those with a continuous taper from the butt to the tip, and these tend to have most movement in the top half of the rod; indeed, one manufacturer has marketed a style of rod with what seems to be almost excessive movement in the tip.

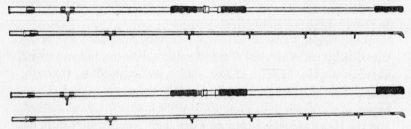

In slightly exaggerated style, the top rod shows taper dropping away from the ferrule in both joints. In the lower rod, the taper is seen to be progressive from butt, through ferrule, to the tip—as in conventional rods

Generally, I believe, anglers perfect their technique with a particular design of rod and spend the rest of their time promoting that design, without ever having tried another, but, whatever design you favour, your decision should be tempered by the 'feel' of the action. A rod that is too stiff will be unable to generate sufficient power for really effective casting, and one that is too soft, or floppy, will lose its casting power in excessive bend and sluggish return to the unflexed state. It is difficult to describe exactly how the action should feel in a good rod, but with the right casting weight it should bend easily—not excessively—and you will be able to sense a reserve of power for use if the need should arise.

REELS

There are several designs of reels, the less common models being variations or adaptations of centre-pins, but to all intents and purposes there are only two of interest to the beach caster—the fixed-spool reel and the multiplier.

While the fixed-spool reel proper is a perfectly adequate casting tool, the majority of experienced beach casters favour the multplier as the ideal reel for great distances when using high breaking-strain lines in conjunction with heavy leads. The very design of the fixed-spool reel is perhaps its own limitation, for although thick line—as it must be for sea angling—slips easily over the lip of the spool in the initial stages and comes off smoothly for the first 40 or 50yd, after this amount of line has left the reel the drag on the remaining line increases badly. The more line that goes out, the lower the level of line still on the reel and the greater the friction as this line is pulled up over the lip. Reduce this resistance, and obviously the lead will travel much further.

With a fixed-spool reel, the lightest possible line commensurate with the weight to be cast should be used, and it is essential that this line should fill the spool right up to the spool lip. To stand the shock of casting, 15ft of high-breaking-strain line, say 10lb higher than the main reel line, should be used as a casting leader, and this will enable one to use heavy leads. Indeed, once the strong leader has taken the initial shock of casting, the light line will offer comparatively less resistance to the wind than a higher breaking-strain line, and less drag to the sea. But for really long casting with weights of over 4oz, there is no doubt that the multiplier, in skilled hands, will cast further.

The fixed-spool reel comes into its own for the angler who has just not the time to learn or the aptitude to use the multiplier, for casts of 80yd or so are quite possible if the spool is correctly filled. Certainly, there is little risk of the shocking 'bird's nest' of line which could result from a multiplier in a beginner's hands.

Very simple centre-pin reels *can* be used for long casting, but considerable expertise is required, and the path towards such expertise is often long and troubled.

Multipliers, really, are the ideal, all-round reels for this form of angling. Many models are currently available, ranging from those with air fins, magnetic brakes, and ball-bearing clutch systems, to plain uncluttered, free-running reels. Various refinements can help to stop the reel from over-runs, but it should be

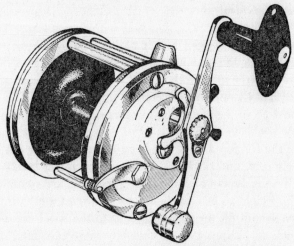

A multiplier is the ideal, all-round reel for beach casting

borne in mind that any restriction upon the drum must inevitably affect the distance to which the cast will go. It is the author's belief that a plain, free-running reel, controlled only by an educated thumb, is the best tool for distance casting.

Some multipliers are very wide between the plates, designed to carry between 250 and 300yd of high-breaking-strain line, but there seems little point in loading a reel with line which will seldom, if ever, be used. Once you have made your big cast, say, 125yd, you will have expended almost as much line as you will need and, while a reserve of line is necessary for

emergencies, it is improbable that one will ever need anywhere
near double that casting length. In the beach-casting situation,
it would be a formidable task indeed for the average angler to
control any sizeable fish at such a range. All that unnecessary
line on the wide spool is just unnecessary weight, and as the
cast begins, this spool weight sets up a heavy 'fly-wheel' action
which could shatter one's hopes of distance in a tangled mass of
line.

Multipliers with narrow drums tend to be much easier to
handle, for the line flowing off from edge to edge across the
drum over a smaller area does not cause as much side-to-side
drag as on the wider drum. Larger, heavier drums also need
more energy to be brought into movement and, once moving,
require considerable control as the lead flies through its trajectory. Because the problem is magnified if the drum is made of
metal and is therefore heavy, one should choose reels carrying
drums made of lightweight plastic material.

Narrow reels with plastic drums start revolving easily as the
low weight inertia is overcome very quickly, and only a little, light
thumb control is necessary until the final stages of the cast. The
spool gives line quickly at the beginning of the cast, as it must,
for it is then that tremendous energy is imparted to the lead
by the rod. Once the lead has settled into flight and is beginning
to slow under the resistance of the length of line following it
through the air, the reel does not have to provide line so quickly.
With line coming off a fast-decreasing core diameter, the narrow
drum is paying out less line—and this is exactly what is needed
and can be easily controlled by the lightest thumb pressure.

It is important to ensure that the reel you are about to buy
has good bearings which hold the drum snugly and without
wobble but, regardless of the model you choose, and whether
expensive or inexpensive, its casting performance will be influenced to a tremendous extent by the manner in which the line
is laid upon the drum. Line bulked to one side or piled upon
a large knot will affect the balance of the drum as it revolves

at high speed and, quite often, line will catch upon a knot, turn
on itself against the drum, and start the most involved tangle.

Lay the line evenly and neatly across the drum when loading
a reel with new line, and avoid large knots when attaching the
line. During the course of fishing, attention to detail will keep the
reel in good casting order. Guide the line on to the spool during
retrieving, using the forefinger and thumb of the hand uppermost
on the rod and, when pulling against a snag, take the weight off
the drum by grasping the line forward of the reel. After a heavy
fish, or a bad snag, has caused the line on the drum to bite down
upon itself, strip the line off the reel until it flows freely and
this will ensure your next cast comes off smoothly.

Plastic spools were at one time very vulnerable to breakage
from the pressure of nylon monofilament, but the advent of fibreglass reinforced spools has almost completely eradicated this
weakness. However, do not risk throwing the drum out of balance
by over-working it under excessive pressure. After tension on
the drum, free the line and wind it back coned slightly in the
centre of the drum. This will allow the final contraction to take
place without excessive outward pressure on the side flanges.

THE LINE

For general-purpose beach casting, there can be little doubt that
nylon monofilament is most widely used and is the most suitable.
It is a line which lends itself well to distance casting, offering
comparatively little resistance to wind and current and being
quite durable if treated with care. *Care* is merely relative in this
case, for, provided one observes certain precautions, monofilament
is found to be extremely tough.

As long as the diameter of a good monofilament remains constant it will give good service, but undue strain upon a length
of line will stretch it out, reduce diameter in parts, and lower
the breaking strain. Nicks and abrasions in the line, from pulling
over rocks or from tangling about the reel, will automatically

rule out any originally quoted breaking strain. Contact with a lighted cigarette, or even the heat in proximity to a cigarette, can cause unsuspected weakness in nylon—until it is put under strain! Twists in a line also cause weakness, and are invariably imparted to the line by the use of terminal tackle which does not incorporate swivels. Line may be stretched and weakened at a hook eye or trace connection by knots pulled too tight—and one should always remember that even the perfectly tied knot must necessarily lower the quoted breaking strain!

The ideal beach-casting lead must be something of a compromise. It will be required to take the bait out the greatest distance that you can cast, and having done that, to keep the bait on the sea-bed roughly where you want it to stay. For pure distance, a pear-shaped lead is, aerodynamically, the most suitable, for leads which do not have the bulk of the weight situated well forward in the nose tend to be ungainly to cast, and to turn over and over in flight. Unfortunately, the pear-shaped lead cannot double-up with holding properties once the cast is made, so that while such a lead may prove adequate much of the time, it is really at its best in flight.

The spiked lead holds well, almost *too* well, at times, on almost any nature of seabed, but it does not cast as well as one would wish, and, when the moment comes to strike, it will sometimes dig into the seabed and sap the power of the strike. In the author's experience, the requirements are well met by leads commonly known as pyramid or torpedo-shaped. These have the weight situated well forward for smooth casting, but have flat sides which offer a reasonable purchase on most types of bed.

The actual weight of a lead must also be considered carefully. Many anglers believe that a heavy lead, without other considerations, will automatically make for a longer cast, but the casting weight must relate to the breaking strain of line. Attempt to

E

throw out a lead which is too heavy for the breaking strain of line, and the chances are great that this lead will break off at the first jerk in the casting movement. Working on the assumption that one is using a main reel line of 18lb b.s., the casting weight should not exceed 4oz. When conditions call for the use of a heavier lead, a shock-absorbing length of higher-breaking-strain line should be attached to the reel line as a casting leader. You may well get away with casting excessively heavy leads on line below strain, but the line is still taking tremendous shocks along its length each time you cast and weakness will not become apparent until the line is under strain. It could result in the loss of a good fish.

The strength of monofilament lying in its diameter, strong, large-diameter line will need a comparatively heavy lead to cut through wind and to keep the bait in place against the push of the sea. Ideally, one should keep casting weight down as low as fishing conditions will allow, while bearing in mind that a thick, strong line presents considerable resistance to current and an ultra-light lead may soon be washed back up on to the beach.

Leads tend to spin in flight, or turn over and over as they are moved over the seabed, and this lead movement imparts twist to the line. Obviate this by ensuring that terminal tackle is set on swivels or, ideally, if you make your own leads, incorporate a swivel as the securing point of the lead. Invariably, fishing is made more sensitive if the lead is free-running, rather than being tied into the line.

TERMINAL TACKLE

Terminal tackle is a swivelled trace holding the casting lead and hook. It has to travel out to where the fish are found, with the bait intact and, once there, lead the fish to believe that what it carries is merely another natural feature of the seabed. To travel well in flight and to achieve its end product, it must be neat and simple.

The brass contraptions popularly used in the past are best left

to the art galleries of this age, for the ideal terminal tackle should
be devoid of anything which is not absolutely functional, should
be uncomplicated, and sensitive. If one could fish with just a free
line and a hook, that would be the most sensitive rig you could find.

Unfortunately, however, one needs a lead to get the bait out
and swivels to stop that lead from weakening and restricting
the line, and, once you have the hook and bait, that is *all* you

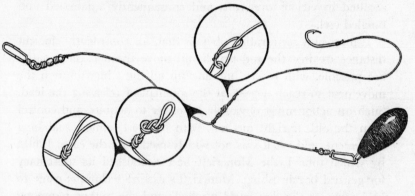

A simple terminal rig. Insets show method of tying 'soft' boom and
attaching hook length

need. The technical-looking, so-called refinements employed by
some anglers are, in most cases, totally unnecessary and, indeed,
it is the author's belief that two hooks on a trace is one hook too
many. The best sport comes from playing a fish at the end
of a line, not in attempting to catch as many fish as one can at
one throw, and the freshwater angler demonstrates that sport
can be enjoyed to the full with a single hook. That second hook
might also be regarded as a potential anchor, dragging over the
seabed behind a running fish.

CASTING TECHNIQUE

At one time, the traditional method of casting was for the caster,
standing upright, to face the sea with the rod held back over one

shoulder, then to punch forward with the hand uppermost on the rod and pull in with the hand on the lower butt. This generated tremendous power in the rod over a relatively small arc, a power which could send the bait out a long distance, but as it also required fine discernment and almost continuous control over the reel it was the very devil of a method to master. Invariably, for all but the most skilled, two casts out of three resulted in vicious over-runs and consequently a jammed and tangled reel.

It must now seem rather obvious that, for consistently efficient distance casting, the rod tip should move through the greatest arc possible, with power building up all the while through the movement to reach a peak at the moment of releasing the lead. Such an action must obviously be easier to acquire and control than the old, upright method, with its short, almost snatching movement, and yet it was not widely used until the early 1960s, by which time Leslie Moncrieff had established its supremacy for general beach fishing. Moncrieff's casting technique came to be known as the 'lay back' method, and the author is among many beach casters who consider it to be the method best suited to the average angler of normal physique. Those who seek distance by the easiest possible course will not go wrong if they perfect the 'lay back' method. It is as follows :

The caster's right hand grasps the top of the butt to enable the thumb to rest upon the reel, and the left hand goes to the bottom of the butt, just forward of the rubber button. Now the rod is laid well back with the right arm extended, reel downwards. The body leans to the right, too, with the weight on the right leg, and the caster looking back to the rod tip. The body should be relaxed.

Just before movement commences, the left hand on the bottom of the butt is raised slightly to give as great an arc as possible for the rod tip to cover. Now the movement proper starts, with the right hand beginning to push the rod, the body beginning to pivot, with weight coming on to the left foot, and the left hand coming down to the left side of the body. The left hand does not pull the bottom of the butt down as such, but rather acts as a guide down the body while the right hand generates power.

The right hand begins to step up the power, the left hand straightening around knee level, the body pivoting to the front, the weight coming fully onto the left leg. Now the right arm extends to impart the full power of the shoulder, the left hand brings the bottom of the butt in, outside of the thigh, and the body leans into putting maximum power into the rod for the moment of release. The cast is completed as the bend in the rod flicks the lead powerfully forward, the tip following the line of flight.

The tip of the rod should travel through its arc to the right of the body, rather than being a directly overhead movement, and, if the cast has been made correctly, little or no thumb control need be exercised over the reel until the lead has reached the height of its trajectory and begins to fall.

Perhaps the best understanding of this casting technique will come from careful study of the accompanying illustration, but there are minor points to be considered. Exactly how far one leans

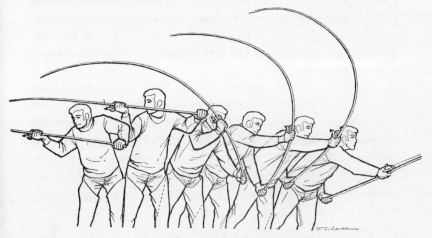

The 'lay back' style of casting

back or into the cast, or the positioning of the feet, depends much
upon the individual. Rather than adopt what feels to be a restricting position through compliance with the positions in the diagram,
seek a compromise which relaxes the body and makes for comfort.
As for the guiding left hand, this does not pull down to aid
the power in the action, but is purely a *guiding* hand to control
the rod while the right hand generates force. The real technique
behind consistently successful casting performance is co-ordina-
tion, with the movement starting slow and easy, building up
power along the way until the whole body has contributed to
the whip-like climax.

Having considered the movement leading up to the release of
the lead, we must now consider the crucial moment of release.
Remove the thumb from the reel too soon and the lead may
rocket vertically upwards, or veer along the beach as a very
lethal weapon. Remove the thumb too late and the lead will fall
short, perhaps a mere rod's length to the front, in the shingle—
and then you may have a fine mess on the reel to sort out!

Many anglers have a short phrase which starts with the cast
and ends with the lead being released, and Moncrieff once told
me that he says 'Get out of it'; the word 'get' starting the cast,
and 'it' prompting release. However, I believe that many anglers
will know instinctively when to release the lead, and this will
happen automatically as the rod comes out of compression. I
would suggest that, initially, the tyro tries to gauge the moment
of release instinctively and lets events take their course, rather
than fall into the trap of trying to co-ordinate the cast to the
timing of a short sentence. If the feel of the cast itself does not
suggest when best to release the lead, then one can resort to the
'get out of it' routine.

CHAPTER FOUR

Boat Fishing

TO many anglers, sea fishing means boat fishing. These anglers, thousands upon thousands of them, travel the many miles from inland industrial towns every weekend to go afloat, content to put their faith on a chance of sport in the hands of a boatman. The charterboats ply for hire out of many harbours and, such is the popularity of this form of angling, some of these boats are employed the year around, full time, for sport fishing. The skippers learn the productive marks of their own particular coastlines, many build national reputations on the knowledge they acquire, and so the faith of many weekend anglers is invariably well justified.

Many of these skippers are well-known angling personalities, running boats with names as well known as their own, and often the mention of a certain boat is alone sufficient to evoke thoughts of certain marks and particular species of fish. Such association promotes the livelihood of these skippers and, not surprisingly, they are very much concerned with the welfare and safety of their passengers as well as the degree of sport they are able to provide. Very few skippers let down the high standards of the professional seaman, and the few that do, do not reign long. Inevitably, the cream of the sport-fishing fleets of various coasts can be contacted through the advertising columns of the angling press.

Hire fees vary from area to area, but the scale of charges is generally constant within an area, with seasonal fluctuations. Many anglers book a boat on a party basis, sharing the expenses of the day—transport, food, bait, etc,—with a group of friends, and this, particularly when the group has established a good relationship over a period of time with the boatman and his craft, can lead to the best of all worlds.

For the occasional, casual tripper afloat, there may be risk of hiring a place on an unsafe boat with an inexperienced or inconsiderate skipper, but these are generally about only when the season is at its peak, or excessive publicity has been given to a particular coast and when other, known boats are fully booked. There is virtually no way for the tyro to know what he is to be faced with before arriving at his destination and appraising the situation for himself, although one may sometimes find a recommended boat through one's local tackle dealer.

The fishing-tackle dealer, in any town, is invariably at the centre of the angling grape-vine and the holder of a fund of information. He hears all about that fabulous cod catch in so-and-so's boat off such-and-such a place, the comfort, or the bait facilities. He also hears about boatmen with poor equipment, who do not turn out at the appointed time, are slow to find productive marks, and want to get back into port again as soon as possible. If your local tackle dealer is a good one, the chances are great that you will be able to get reliable information on coastal fishing prospects, and on where to book a boat.

Once you have your place in a boat and have been taken out to the area's productive mark, exactly what facilities your boatman provides much depends upon the manner of man he is. Some boatmen tend to 'switch-off' in more ways than one, once the engine has been stopped, and sit back to watch the proceedings. Others cut bait, dispense advice on the fishing freely, gaff or net large fish, and keep the tea flowing—and such men are just like good angling companions. All in all, it is a case of taking pot luck in finding a combination of good skipper and angler, and happily this combination is not as rare as might seem.

To a very great extent, the success of a day's outing can depend upon the boat's skipper. The experienced man will know the chances of a mark producing fish, should know whether time is being wasted over a particular mark, and should be able to put the boat over another mark and find sport. He will know all about the rock ledges which yield bream or pollack, of wrecks which hold big conger and ling, and the shingle shoals which can turn up turbot or giant skate. Your part will come in tackling these fish; the skipper's part lies in putting you in a position to do so. While an angler may be comparatively naïve yet still catch fish, he will catch them only through the boatman's skill. But the finest angler in the world cannot catch fish where there are none.

It can prove much to your benefit to respect the judgement of the boatman, particularly if you are a stranger to the district, for while the average person tends to view the sea as a great expanse of featureless water, the discerning seaman, or angler, knows that different species live in special little environments within the main environment. Along the road to such knowledge a lot of hours will have been spent studying charts, an understanding will have been gained of the various traces of seabed brought up on anchor and chain, and a pretty through knowledge of fish will have been acquired. You may now appreciate that successful boat fishing is something of a team effort, with the boatman the mainstay of the team.

BOAT-FISHING TACKLE

Boat fishing, in the author's experience, cannot be fully enjoyed as a pastime with one set of basic tackle. Despite what some tackle manufacturers would have us believe, there is no such thing as general-purpose tackle. Whatever scale a rod and reel might be, it could not hope to provide sport with bream, bass, pollack and codling and then be brought into play with similar effect against big cod and ling from deep marks, or giant conger and skate which, at a very conservative estimate, could reach weights in the regions of 60lb.

Often one cannot successfully use more than one rod at a time, especially when the fish are really 'on', but two outfits are essential to allow one to play the field, and the use of a particular outfit will be decided by the nature of a mark and the species of fish that mark is likely to yield.

Boat rods are made of tubular or solid-glass fibre, in one continuous length from tip to rubber button, or in two pieces, with the ferrule normally joining the rod length at the butt. Some manufacturers still produce rods of built-cane, and these can be superb, but nothing stands up to salt water and the abuse a rod can receive at sea like glass fibre.

At first, it might seem that solid glass must obviously be stronger than tubular glass, but, unless one goes to extremes, and disregarding smashes and stresses imposed through negligence, there is little between the two forms other than weight. Indeed, a subtle difference in action can be felt between a solid rod and a tubular rod, particularly if the tubular rod has a tapered wall. Unless you shut your tubular rod in the car door, or stamp on it, you will find that for general boat fishing you can do with tubular glass all that you could do with solid glass, and probably with less effort.

Boat rods are short rods, as they must be for convenient winching action and wielding within the confines of a boat, and range between 5 and 8ft in length. The lighter rods for the free-swimming, normally smaller fishes are invariably the longest, the extra-powerful, short rods being reserved for the bottom-dwelling leviathans. Light rods will normally be furnished with comparatively light rod rings and winch fittings, while the extra-powerful rod will feature heavy-duty rod rings and a pulley end ring, and securing devices on the winch fitting.

The light rod with a tapered glass wall may well be sufficiently versatile in its action to react immediately to the slight knocking of a flounder, and yet still be powerful enough to control the run of a tope, but beyond that it will not go. One wants to fish lightly to enjoy the very best of sport, but still *lightly* is a relative term, and light tackle should be read as the lightest equipment which prevailing conditions and the species involved will allow.

The extra-powerful rod will, quite apart from handling the actual weight of a big conger or skate, even shark, be required to cope with the mere mechanics of this sort of fishing, and there

A medium-sized multiplier with a sensible handle

must be power to winch up leads which could weigh 1lb from deep-water marks. In a fast tide race, even this can seem an exhausting task if the rod does not have enough 'back' in it. Depending upon the size of fish you have in mind, your big rod will need a test curve of between 15 and 20lb.

A medium-size multiplier will complement the light rod ideally, and the best of these reels have sensibly large handles. In this form of sea angling, one just cannot have too much line, and the weight of this on the drum is unimportant, for there is no casting as such. My own light boat reel is loaded to capacity with 20lb b.s. line, and, while this may seem to be too light by many standards, I have, on several occasions, found no difficulty in beating fish weighing over 30lb. For those wanting a more dramatic example, Dutton Everington—the boatman at Littlehampton, in Sussex—is on record as having boated tope weighing up to 60lb on 20lb line. However, if one is to fish with light line—and I have found occasion to use 15lb b.s. line in the past—then this should be of one continuous length rather than being made up from two or three lengths tied on from separate 100yd spools. When you buy your line, stipulate connected spools.

A multiplier can be used successfully with the heavy rod, but

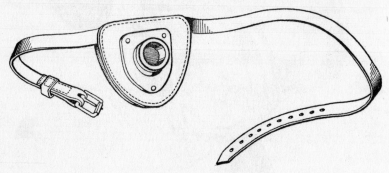

The 'Efgeeco' groin protector

it would have to be a big, large-capacity reel to carry the necessary line, that is, a minimum of 60lb b.s. Because multipliers of any size tend to be heavy reels and are situated on top of the rod, there is a considerably tiring side-to-side movement as one winds against a fish, and thus a harness is essential for the big outfit. For those yet to become addicted to the fads and fancies which beset experienced anglers, a centre-pin, 6in in diameter, will prove much easier to handle. Certainly it will carry more line than the average large multiplier, and can provide a fine feeling of direct contact with the quarry.

For those contemplating serious boat fishing, a groin protector is an important accessory. It will provide a safe fulcrum for the rod butt at all times, make all the difference between comfort and possible injury, and is a necessary item of tackle in a lengthy battle with a big fish. In fact, for those anglers intending to specialise with the larger species of fish, the groin protector is an essential, rather than a refinement.

CHAPTER FIVE

The Boat Fisher's Quarry

COD

FEW fish cause as much excitement in the angling world as the cod which arrive off British waters in winter. In fact, the author has met several people content to fish only during the cod months, in lashing rain and biting cold, men who are anglers only when the winter draws them to ports like Newhaven to go afloat in search of cod.

Happily for many, the cod is not a discerning feeder. It takes almost anything which is edible, some things which are not, and there is no doubt about when it takes a bait. A rush at the bait invariably results in the fish hooking itself, and so one seldom needs to strike as such but rather to lift the rod in a controlled movement to ensure that the hook is set. When very large hooks are employed, it pays to take no chances and to strike hard. Having set the hook, you keep the rod tip high to absorb the shocks of a plunging fish, giving line only if the fish is really big and retrieving with a pumping action.

Tackle rigs should be as simple as possible, with whatever weight prevailing conditions demand, and these rigs can run to extremes, for cod fishing is a pastime of variance. Early in the season it may be almost flat seas, with codling of 5 or 6 lb coming readily to the bait, and then, after October, rough seas and howling winds, and great fish of 20, 30, and even 40lb.

Many anglers get by with one standard size of hook, whatever conditions, but popular hook sizes are 4/0 for the early codling

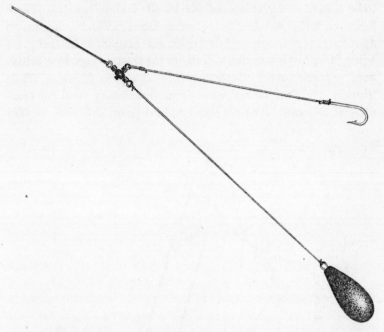

A simple but effective cod rig. The line from lower eye of swivel should
   be of lower breaking strain than the reel line to make a 'rotten bottom'

and 6/0 or 8/0 for the winter giants. For these big fish, with
their huge, gaping mouths, it would be difficult to think of a
conventional hook which would be too large, but one has to bear
in mind that the large hook has a maximum holding power only
when it has been powerfully set, and the larger the hook the more
force required to set it. I have seen many cod lost when a big
hook has torn from a light purchase in the mouth while the fish
has been on the surface.

Baits may be chosen from marine worms, various shellfish,
cuttle, fish cuttings, or small, whole fish set on the trace with a
baiting needle. Artificial baits of various kinds can also be used,
and the best of these are heavy metal lures.

The author was introduced to the effectiveness of what seemed to be monstrous metal lures off Reykjavik, Iceland, in 1959. These lures, virtually just lengths of scrap metal and anything up to 10in long, very heavy and dull coloured, accounted for cod averaging 30lb, but it was difficult, to say the least, to convince British angling friends of the effectiveness of such a piece of metal. While 'rippers' and 'murderers' have been successfully used by commercial fishermen for over one hundred years, it is only in very

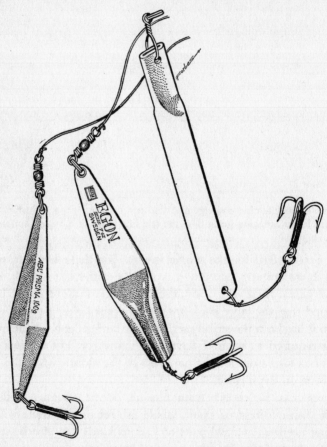

Three styles of 'pirk'. The ABU 'Prisma' as conventionally sold, the 'Egon' —with nylon hook link, and an improvisation from metal piping

recent years that anglers have begun to appreciate the merits of
the more refined versions of such lures. These lures are now
known as 'pirks', and at least one firm markets them for cod
fishing.

The method of use is simple but effective, and the British
record rod-caught cod of 46lb from the Firth of Clyde was caught
on a metal lure. The lure—it could weigh anything from 3 to
10oz—is lowered to the seabed and then line is retrieved to leave
it dangling a few feet clear of the bottom. Now the rod tip is
raised and lowered continuously to impart movement to the lure,
and the more erratic the movement, the better the chances of
fish. In particularly rocky areas there can be extensive tackle
losses, and shop-bought lures—at anything up to 30s a time—
are not cheap. To reduce the risk, one can tie a length of nylon,
lower than the breaking strain of the reel line, from the split-
ring below the lure to the hook. Then, if the lure is snagged in
rough ground, it can be pulled free with only the loss of the
hook.

TOPE

This is the average angler's big game fish, a true shark, every bit
as fierce and predatory as the conventional shark, but often a
better sporting proposition. It is a fish of summer months, of flat
seas and balmy days, but it is also, in the author's experience, a
fish of unpredictable mood.

Tope tend to hunt in packs, on one day savaging fish after
fish that is brought to the boat—even snatching at hooked fish
on the surface—and, on another day, running time after time
with an intended fish-bait but rejecting it for no apparent reason.
Invariably, the days on which tope strike fish after fish without
apparent caution are the days when one is catching mackerel or
bream on ultra-light tackle. The tope seems most cautious on
the days when one is waiting over a tope bait.

While tope can run to very large sizes, a big fish in terms of
everyday fishing might well be between 35 and 40lb. Larger

F

fish are not really uncommon, but still not so common as to warrant the use of excessively strong tackle, which rules out sport with small and medium-size fish. For the general run of tope fishing, the light boat outfit will be admirable and will still offer a sporting chance of beating the occasional big fish.

Tope fishing is somewhat standardised, but ingenuity in presenting a bait on the most resistance-free rig will pay dividends. Considering, however, that one is fishing comparatively light, there must be no weak links in the tackle chain, the reel must be filled to capacity and all the knots sound.

Those intending to specialise to some extent with tope will need lengthy traces of plastic-covered wire to withstand the abrasive qualities of the tope's flanks, for this coarseness could well weaken nylon line dangerously. While I have successfully landed medium-size tope on nylon traces, I would not like to state that this could be done consistently, or even occasionally, where big fish are concerned. I have used high-breaking-strain nylon for traces in the belief that, if the tope is going to bite through a trace, the fact that the trace is wire is not going to stop it, and I think this is a reasonable assumption. Neither have I experienced tope wrapping themselves up in the trace, a theory which has traditionally called for the use of very long, sometimes unmanageable traces. Traces between 4 and 6ft long should be quite adequate to counter any risk of line fraying. Where wire is used, this should be very supple, and the use of connected links of stiff wire—piano wire was very popular at one time!—in my experience, reduces chances of a take.

At the business end of the trace, attach a hook from size 6/0 to 10/0, depending on the size of fish-bait to be used, and ensure that the hook is as sharp as possible. Rather than depend upon the sharpness of shop-bought hooks, cultivate the habit of honing them to a point prior to fishing. I always do this once the tackle is assembled and check after every retrieve, for fine points tend to bend easily, even on shingle.

Tie in a box swivel 3ft up the trace, and a link swivel where

THE BOAT FISHER'S QUARRY

the trace joins the reel line. Some anglers advocate the use of several swivels in the trace, but it might be as well to remember that every join in the trace is a potential weakness.

When tope are known to be working near the surface, one may float fish, or drift out a bait on a leadless rig. With a float rig, use a float which has a line channel through the centre rather than the old, *Fishing Gazette* type of float which pegs to the line. Then, once the tope has run off a considerable distance with the bait, the strike is made *through* the float rather than being muffled by the resistance of the pegged float against the water.

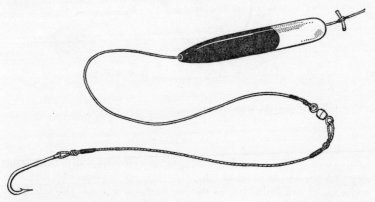

Float tackle incorporating a 4ft, 50lb wire trace. A big-game swivel prevents float running on to trace. Channel floats are best home-made, although ingenuity suggests use of polythene containers and balloons

With the leadless rig, one merely attaches a trace to the reel line and allows the bait to stream in the current, giving line to keep the bait down as far as possible up to a given distance. The author has enjoyed considerable success in the Solent by casting ahead of the boat, paying out slack line and allowing the bait to travel deep until rising astern of the boat. However, this causes considerable wear and tear on the bait, which should be checked carefully.

When one is speculating, it is probably best to leger a bait on the bottom, or well down in the water. The weight of lead required will depend upon prevailing conditions and the state of the water, but in any event the lead should not be tied directly into the reel line but attached so as to offer the least resistance to a fish running with the bait. The standard method is a sliding boom—either a Kilmore or Clements boom—with a line-stop to prevent the boom from fouling and jamming the swivels on the trace.

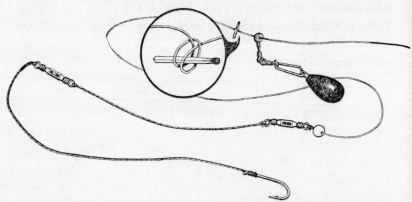

Sliding leger rig for tope incorporating 6ft swivelled trace with bead as line stop. To stream out a really long, free line, the lead may be held back and a matchstick hitched on to the line as shown in inset. The matchstick breaks on the strike

Well-proven baits for tope are fresh mackerel, mounted complete or used in fillets, herrings, sprats, and small flat-fish. While old baits may have accounted for the occasional tope, it is best to get the freshest bait available. If one is short of bait-fish, one can economise by cutting slender, lengthy fillets, but these fillets must be tied to the hook. However one presents the bait, the point of the hook should always be showing to allow of maximum penetration on the strike.

Once the tackle is out, release the reel drum and hold the line back under pressure from the thumb. Bites may be felt as a pluck at the rod tip or a gentle pull. At the first indication of a bite, release the drum and allow the tope to run unhindered. Tope do not *always* run with a bait, but it is the general rule rather than the exception. How far they will run cannot be determined for certain. Possibly the size of bait affects the issue, a small bait prompting the fish to stop after a short run, and a large bait making for a lengthy run. Anyway, allow the line to run out unchecked until it stops of its own accord, then engage the reel and strike. Bear in mind that you have to set a large hook into your fish, which may be 50 or 60yd distant, and so the rod should go right over the shoulder in a powerful sweep. If the strike should feel in any way muffled, make a second strike, but this time bear in mind that your fish will be speeding away and that if you strike too hard this time you may cause a breakage. Resort to a second strike only if the initial strike did not feel firm—few things in fishing can be as frustrating as a tope shedding the hook after a short but furious battle through poor contact on the strike, or through the hook-hold of a good strike being loosened by a second unnecessary strike.

If the tope runs just a few yards, do not strike immediately. Invariably it will run again after a short pause, and the strike should come after the next stoppage. When tope are feeding well, frequent short runs resulting in blanks on the strike generally indicate that something is amiss with the tackle rig. Do not hesitate to change rigs or to modify your tackle. It could make all the difference between catching fish and frustration.

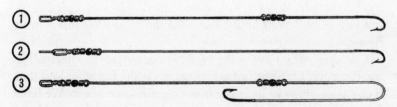

Three alternatives: (1) 12 inches of 50lb wire to 36 ins 50lb nylon, with link swivel to reel line. (2) 48 inches 50lb wire with link swivel to reel line. (3) Conventional 6ft wire trace to link swivel

Tope take many years to attain large sizes, but often this is negated by thoughtless action on the part of the angler and regretted afterwards. Where the waterline may easily be reached from the gunwale, try to boat your fish by swinging them inboard by hand. It is not as difficult or as dangerous as it sounds, and adds spice to the outing. More important, it allows one to return fish relatively unharmed. When high off the water, or attached to a very large tope which one fears losing, the gaff is undoubtedly the most efficient, but unfortunately the most lethal implement.

CONGER EELS

With the strike, the rod went right over into its battle arc, and then nothing happened, there was just this seemingly immovable force down there in the dark water keeping my rod pulled over. For a while it was stalemate, and then the jag-jag-jag began with tremendous power and when I answered with strain there came a force which I could not check. A frighteningly powerful, quick force, that smashed the rod down onto the gunwale with a crack. I had made contact with my first conger.

Conger fishing is a pastime of challenge. The tackle must be strong, very strong, and, if the eeel is big, so must be the angler. The eels are encountered on the seabed, in the fissures of rock formations and the craggy entanglements of wrecks. They may not range far from the security of these places, sometimes merely extending themselves to reach out for food and, once contact has been made, they tend to retire immediately into their lair. It is a case of pull devil, pull baker, and the conger has much in its favour.

One does not set out with, say *light* conger tackle, anticipating small conger. One sets out with conger tackle, full stop, and that tackle is as strong in its weakest link as one can make it. We have fairly conclusive proof that conger eels reach weights of 100lb, perhaps more, and all the signs point to the really big fish coming from deepwater marks. You may well catch very small and even medium-size conger from the shore on relatively light tackle, but you will not do it consistently from deep-water rock or wreck marks. There is a very considerable physical problem in lifting a 40lb fish from its hold on the seabed, and you need the tackle to back you up. There is no finesse. You bend into the fish right from the start and you 'keep it coming'.

The large outfit comes into use now, with the big reel holding line of a minimum of 60lb breaking strain. We are considering our standard outfits for boat fishing, but if one wants to specialise in the pursuit of big conger, then a minimum breaking strain of 80lb is preferable. Our standard reel may be filled with mono-

Large forged hook direct to 12in length of 100lb wire. A further swivel may be wired to the hook eye, and trace knots should be backed up by varnished whippings

fil and, although it will stretch, one can get away with this. However, braided terylene or braided nylon are better suited to this deep-water power work.

Conventional conger hooks are swivel-eyed and, while I have heard anglers tell of the hook pulling out of the swivel hold, I have always found them to be quite adequate. For those seeking the really big conger, it might be as well to use big, forged hooks and attach them to plain swivels by a short length of wire. Hook sizes, according to bait and what size of conger one is after, range from 4/0 to 10/0.

The trace, of necessity, is cable-laid steel wire, of the same breaking strain as the reel line, or even slightly higher. This trace should be swivelled, with strong swivels—but bear in mind that the more swivels one incorporates the greater the likelihood of introducing weakness into the rig. In my experience, a short, strong trace with one really good swivel connecting to the reel line is adequate for the general run of eels. I use big-game swivels, but perhaps this is *too* optimistic. Just ensure that swivels are very strong and securely linked.

Link swivels are often advocated for the connecting point of reel line and trace, but one invariably finds it better to cut the line above the swivel rather than fiddle to obtain the release.

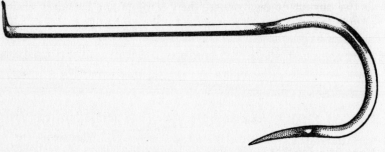

Lash-on gaff heads are essential for conger fishing. Screw-in heads are liable to unscrew as an eel wrenches and twists

More important, in the writer's experience, there seems to be a higher percentage of faulty swivels among link swivels than box or buckle swivels.

Leads should be attached to a comparatively weak length of line to make a 'rotten bottom', and, as one is invariably fishing over rough ground and it is inevitably the lead which fouls, these could be of any scrap metal. Many peculiar things are used as 'sinkers', from lengths of bicycle-chain to piping, but do not choose a type of weight which is liable to snag.

All manner of fresh fish, from sand-eels to mackerel, will tempt conger, and squid is also very good. Convention demands that whole fish be mounted with the head downwards, for it is generally accepted that conger take the bait head-first. However, many conger have been hooked on herring heads with a small length of trailing flesh attached—and the hook passed through the mouth and out the top of the head.

The take of a conger varies. It could be a sudden, long tug, or the line running out constantly, but generally it is an almost imperceptible tremor to the line. If you hold the line between the rod rings when this starts, it feels like something sawing the line.

Exactly when to strike after the indication of a take is open to speculation. Some experienced anglers give lots of time and strike at the first sign of the line moving out, others strike almost immediately. The first school gives the eel lots of time to engulf bait and hook, the second does not want to give the eel a chance of withdrawing into a rock cavity. Whichever method you favour, one would be lucky to make contact with 75 per cent of bites indicated.

The writer's personal fad is for relatively small baits and a few seconds' pause after indication, without further action prompting, before striking. It is felt that run-out or tugging indications are not truly bite forms, but a second-phase action, the initial indication of line tremor having passed unnoticed. This happens because the angler is not concentrating or, less probably, because slack line has ruled out the initial indication.

Once the strike has been made, there is no cause for debate on the following action. Bend into the fish immediately and get it clear of the bottom, if you can. If you cannot lift, then hold, but do not—unless there is a good chance of open ground below —allow the conger line with which to run. You may safely bet, if you do, that it will make straight for a hole in which to lodge, or something upon which it may obtain a purchase, and then you really have problems. Get your eel off the bottom, try to keep it off, and give only enough line to save a breakage.

It is amazing just how much strain you can put on to rod and line, even after it seems that the tackle cannot possibly take any more, and this is best demonstrated in trying to get free of a normal snag—even with light tackle.

Several factors influence your chances of success with conger eels. The size of the eel you are handling, the ground situation from which you are trying to extract it, and the amount of nerve you have in bending into your tackle for the first assault. This presupposes that your tackle is conger tackle in good order.

Once clear of the bottom, the eel's struggle will provide a plunging, scissoring sensation. Then, when this fails, it may start to spiral round and round. That is where the swivels in the trace come into play.

With the conger close to the boat, there is only one *safe* way to land it, and that is with a good, sharp gaff. This should be the lash-on, rather than the screw type, for that spiralling movement could take the gaff head out of the handle. And do not attempt to gaff your eel until it is comfortably within reach. When it is, place the gaff and strike upwards with one movement which will deposit the eel inboard.

Now comes an interesting part. Some anglers maintain that the real fight starts with the eel in the boat, and, if you are a beginner, it is as well to let the boatman complete the gaffing and despatching. Methods of despatch vary from striking the vent region with a heavy implement to plunging a sharp knife into the neck at the base of the skull. In theory it sounds fairly easy, but with a big, lively eel, it can be altogether a different matter. The writer once had to get up into the bows of a dinghy to escape the frantic attempts of an angler to subdue a conger with a hammer—and then plug up a sizeable hole in the bottom, where the angler had 'missed'!

Take a good strong sack with you when you go conger fishing. Hoist your conger over the sack and cut the line above the trace. Don't take any chances, and secure the sack. Once you have got over the excitement, you can decide exactly what you are going to do. However you decide to despatch the eel, and however 'dead' it appears, do not attempt to remove the hook. Conger eels have a nasty habit of coming back to life.

DOGFISH

Experienced sea anglers tend to disregard the various dogfish for sport, and the beginner need not worry about specialised tackle and technique. Dogfish—lesser spotted, greater spotted, smooth-hound, and spurdog—forage for food in shoals which may number thousands, and it is a farily safe bet that, if a shoal is working through your fishing area, you will hook them on whatever tackle you are using.

When dogfish abound, you seldom catch other species, and you can catch dogfish one after another in a monotonous fishing ritual until your arms and shoulders are tired. The only qualification for catching them is that they be there to be caught, and you get them despite your tackle, not because of it. None of the dogfish provides a real fight, even on light tackle, the spurdog being the best of a bad bunch.

The first thing you will notice about a dogfish in the boat is that it is a very lively creature, and then, when you try to get hold of it, that the skin is very rough and rasping. Hold the fish down firmly before retrieving your tackle and you will save your hands from the abrasive quality of the skin. Where spurdog are concerned, keep your hands well clear of the spines at the leading edges of the fins. These can inflict deep wounds if the angler is careless, for they are like bone daggers rather than the thin, conventional spines found in the dorsal fins of some other species.

There is compensation in the fact that fresh dogfish make very good eating.

POLLACK

Large pollack are fine fighting fish, lovers of rocky ledges and crevices in deep water, and a very worthy quarry of the boat angler. Pollack and coalfish are very similar in appearance and are frequently confused with each other, but coalfish are very limited in distribution and most commonly encountered in northern waters.

As pollack tend to hole up near rocks to ambush their prey, rather than to rove about in search of food, the fishing can be rather tricky. Legering with a line laid out over the seabed is normally ruled out because of snags, and so the fishing is generally 'up and down', the rig being run out until it touches bottom and then withdrawn a few feet. A sea swell will often impart movement to the boat which will be carried to the bait below, but otherwise it is almost essential to keep lifting the rod up and down to keep the bait moving.

Feathers, rubber sand-eels, fish strips or small fish baits are very productive when kept on the move, and these baits are best presented on a rig made up with a 'rotten bottom'. This is a length of line weaker than the reel line, to take the lead, not the hook trace! Invariably it is the lead which fouls rocks, and fish which have run into rocks can be retrieved with merely the loss of the lead. Again, all manner of weights can be used to save the expense of losing shop-bought leads.

Several hook permutations are traditionally used for pollack-fishing rigs, but it is the author's feeling that less inconvenience is suffered and more sport enjoyed, if one limits the rig to a one-hook arrangement. Numerous hooks tend to tangle, in and out of the boat, and to get caught up in tough bottom weed when a fish runs through it. So, unless one is interested only in the most fish caught for the least energy expended, strings of feathers or sand-eel lures are best left alone. One should also consider what might happen on the freak chance of a shoal of really large pollack attacking the multi-feather or lure rig, and two, or even three, double-figure fish becoming hooked at one time. If the fish are present, a one-hook rig will improve sport for the discerning angler.

Two factors decide greatly how good the pollack catch will be. Known pollack haunts should be really well known, and the boat situated to allow tackle to get as close as possible to the ledge-face or outcrops in which the fish are holing up. Having got into position—everything here depending upon the boatman's knowledge and ability—the second factor is the handling of the tackle. Do not indulge in the pastime of leaving the tackle to fish for itself—all too common in sea angling—but try to impart as much movement and apparent life to the end tackle as possible. Work at it, trying to keep the bait fluttering and jerking, rather

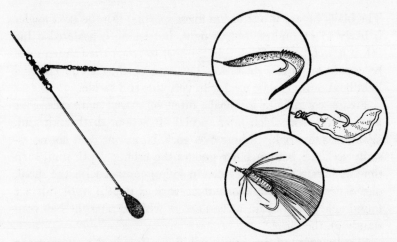

Terminal rig incorporating 'rotten bottom' from three-way swivel. Insets show various effective pollack baits, all of which rely upon jerky movement

than fall into an automatic up-and-down movement, and think in terms of the *movement* of the bait, rather than the actual bait, attracting your fish.

In this type of fishing, as in all manner of lure fishing, once one has assembled the necessary tackle, it is the attitude of mind which is of prime importance. One often hears of old so-and-so down the coast, reputed to be very lucky and able to catch fish in a bucket of water. This is the sort of man who consistently takes fish, and often when other anglers are talking of the fish being 'off', the tide wrong, and such things. He is the sort of man who keeps his rod in his hands, working the bait or lure all the time, even when there have been no fish for several hours and the rest of the company have resorted to talking and leaving their rods unattended.

By all means rely upon the expertise of a boatman to find the fish, but do not expect him to catch them for you as well.

BLACK BREAM

The black bream is one of the finest sporting fish the boat angler is likely to encounter, full of fight, but small, considered a big fish if it weighs 4lb. Such fish, if one is to enjoy the fishing, must be caught on ultra-light tackle, but, at a pinch, the conventional light boat outfit can be used with very fine end tackle.

Bream congregate in shoals, often of many thousands, over parts of the sea which offer special attractions to the fish and, again, it is invariably fishing over rock. Now, one does not necessarily seek the bottom but regulates the fishing depth until such time as bream are contacted. On losing contact with the shoal, one experiments with the bait at various depths until fish are found again, and again success comes with keeping the bait constantly on the move.

Slender strips of fish, which will flash silver in the water, make ideal baits and are fished on a small hook, say, a size 6, with a

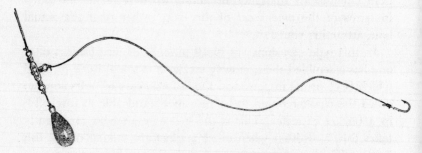

A 4ft trace of 5lb nylon to three-way swivel. Nylon lead link from the lower eye makes a 'rotten bottom' for fishing over rock

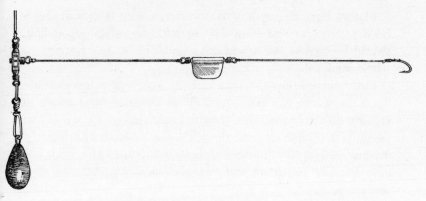

A 6ft trace of 10lb nylon incorporating anti-kink vane

barbed shank to allow baits to be secured. Use only just enough lead to get the bait down to the fish, and, while water conditions will ultimately dictate the amount required, a 1oz pear lead is generally sufficient.

THORNBACK RAY

This ray is probably the one most commonly encountered by British anglers, the common skate being relatively uncommon and a giant which calls for specialised angling. Thornbacks, however, are frequently found over banks of shingle, sand, and mud, in the deeps and inshore, are available in fair numbers and provide some degree of sport on the light boat rig.

Traditional tackle for rays tends to be very heavy but, in the writer's experience, so few large thornback rays are landed in the course of normal sea fishing that the use of this tackle is ruled out. The locale and the size of fish likely to be caught should, of course, control the scale of tackle one would use, but thornbacks are relatively small, require some power to be moved initially, and can normally be quite confidently handled on the standard boat rod and tackle. To veer on the safe side, the angler should be governed by local experience and conditions.

Sliding leger rig, with a nylon-covered wire trace carrying a hook ranging in size from 3/0 to 5/0, depending upon bait, should be used to fish worm baits, small crabs, fish cuttings, or whole small fish.

Once the rod tip indicates a bite, the course of action depends upon the size of bait being used. With worm or fish cuttings, it is fairly safe to assume that the ray has settled over the bait and engulfed it completely, and the strike can be made immediately. With a comparatively large fish-bait, it is best to give slack line after the bite indication and to make the strike when the slack line has gone.

Rays are not active fighters and most of the action experienced is from the play of the water on the shape of the fish. For this reason, even a small ray can seem quite heavy in a fast tide race. The real power has to be applied immediately on the strike, to overcome the suction-like grip of the ray on the seabed, but once off the bottom it is normally just a case of winching, with no line being given. The thornback will be at its liveliest just after it is hauled clear of the seabed.

It is reasonable to assume that the ray is lifted from the bottom with the power of the strike and then does its utmost to get down on to the bed again. It is just when it is trying to do this that the

A very simple sliding leger rig for thornbacks. The lead may run simply on a lead link, Kilmore boom or, better still, a large link swivel

average angler unintentionally helps it. The typical routine is to heave the rod back into the strike, feel the weight of the fish, and then lower the rod tip to start a pumping action. The lowering comes at exactly the right time for the ray, and when the angler starts his pumping he really *does* have to pump, for now the ray is flat on the seabed with wings down.

Instead of watching the rod tip dipping, with the rod resting against the gunwale of the boat, pick the rod up, lower the tip down to the waterline and take up the slack line. Now, make the strike, and the rod will flex into an arc at somewhere around shoulder level. Immediately start taking in line on the reel, but keep the rod coming up. This action should succeed in getting your ray upwards and moving in one almost continuous movement. When you do have to start pumping, you will have gained enough clearance, with luck, to start the upward movement of the rod again without the ray having been able to reach the bottom.

With the conventional strike from the gunwale position, the rod flexes over the head and there is nowhere else for it to travel from there. It would have to be a strong man indeed that could start retrieving line with the rod at the full, backward limit of the strike position, and so the rod has to come down for the pumping action to begin.

The important thing, I believe, is that striking and effort in lifting the ray off the bottom are synchronised into one almost continuous movement, as opposed to a definite strike and then an attempt to lift after giving a couple of feet of line. On the one hand, you are moving a fish and keeping it moving, restricting it from getting fully under way, and thus have the initiative. On the other, you are moving a fish, giving it a fraction of time and slack line, and fighting it when it is fully aware of what is happening and is attempting to take evasive action.

This course of action may be merely one of the fads which experienced anglers tend to adopt, for anglers are funds of what often turns out to be unsubstantiated and illogical 'fact', but I

G

do really believe that refusing to give even the smallest length of slack line immediately after the strike has enabled me to beat fish which have taken a bait on the verge of a snag, and allowed me to take charge before the fish has had time to recover from the surprise of finding that an apparently harmless morsel of food has turned out to be something else. In any event, there can be little doubt that, probably in blind panic, the fish exerts itself most powerfully in immediate response to the strike.

Assuming that tackle is sound, this is the time when the angler should be ready to combat that response, ready to put on pressure that will never allow the fish to start moving as well as it might. Only then does the angler dictate the terms.

This type of action, of course, is intended to cover the playing of only small and medium-size fish, and not the 'unstoppable' giants. Disaster could result from this approach to, say, a huge mako or porbeagle shark, but it is still a fact that the easier time you give a fish, and the more line you let it have, the harder you have to work to get the upper hand and to recover that line.

CHAPTER SIX

Rock Fishing

THE origin of rock fishing goes back to the earliest times, when man first sought the fish of the sea for food. Then the tackle was a length of line with a primitive hook, lowered into dark water surging into rock cavities. Later, it was discovered that a long branch controlled the line better than the extended arm. The long branch eventually became a supple rod, but the evolution of the technique froze there, for it was to be a long, long time before the refinement of a reel was added. Indeed, the long, unjointed rod with a length of line whipped on to the tip was a method, seemingly crude but effective, which persisted in some parts of the British Isles up to about thirty years ago. Elsewhere in the world, particularly on some Mediterranean islands, rock fishing with the fixed line is still practised with very considerable success.

As might be expected, the best of British rock fishing is to be found along rugged, rocky coastlines, although the discerning angler may find sport at many other venues at the full of the tide, just before the day breaks, or the evening settles into dusk. But for consistent sport, the almost certainty, one must turn to the shores of Scotland, western Wales, Ireland, or, perhaps best of all, Devon and Cornwall.

Once you have your venue, that stretch of shoreline with water washing rafts of weed between rocks, success stems not so much from actual techniques and tackle used as from what you learn about the points you are to fish.

Low tide offers a good opportunity to study points which will

99

later be covered by water and, apart from ground level, this may be done from high vantage points on surrounding cliffs. You may better appreciate the deep holes which will be even deeper at the full of the tide, and note the dark patches of weed which may shelter predatory fish, aligning the various different areas with points ashore for later reference. The different characteristics of the shoreline and the seabed, when known, should control one's fishing to a great extent. Thus one may fish a full tide with a working knowledge of what lies beneath the surging water. But high tide is not necessarily the best time for your fishing.

The best time will probably be dictated by the nature of the locale and the amount of activity in that locale. While the wild, remote shore may produce fish at any state of the tide, you may have to seek your fish at first light and again at dusk in areas with a less rugged shore, particularly if the area is frequented by holidaymakers. When you have only the fish to compete with and can creep from rock to rock with stealth, you may find wrasse, pollack, or bass to take your carefully cast bait at low water, and then consistent success comes with putting the type of food which fish expect to find in the kind of place they expect to find it.

While lug worms, rag worms, and other conventional baits inevitably bring fish, the author has experienced his best sport by prospecting for bait in rock pools and under stones in the area to be fished. If one can follow the water down as the tide ebbs, the rock pools along sheltered headlands may be found to contain all manner of small fish, sometimes tiny eels, and invariably shrimps and prawns. Turning over clumps of dense weed and large flat stones may produce further small eels and various blennies. Such creatures are taken almost with abandon by large fish lurking beside rock outcrops and dense weed formations when the water is high, for these are the creatures the fish seek in such locations.

Now it must be emphasised that this chapter deals with rock fishing in its pure sense, rather than the use of rocks as vantage points to cast out long distances to the seabed, and so, discounting the ranging, nomadic fish of the sea, the species encountered by the rock fisher are limited.

THE QUARRY

Wrasse are almost certain to be encountered at most venues, at all times of the day and at all states of the tide, but it is almost equally certain that most of these wrasse will be small, brilliantly

A sliding float rig, with drilled bullet stopped by swan shot, keeps all the terminal weight close to the hook and makes for casting accuracy when necessary. In this case, anticipating big fish, the hook length is made up of 12lb b.s. wire

coloured, and offer little sport. Occasionally, and then usually in remote, deep-water parts, there will be large wrasse, thick-bodied fish which provide the very best of sport. These large fish have formidable teeth, and wire traces are almost a necessity.

Pollack, like wrasse, tend to be generally small, but late in the year the big ones come close inshore, and these, again, provide good sport.

Disregarding the really large wrasse, the rock fisher's ideal fish is the bass. Even in the smaller sizes, it is a fish to test the tackle and reflexes, for it has a tenacity and strength which demand respect. It may be taken on a wide variety of baits and, unlike wrasse and pollack, there is no predictable run of sizes. The bass which takes your bait may be one of a school of small fish, weighing a mere pound or two, or it might be a plump six-pounder. There might just be, in response to a fish-bait fished craftily under the fronds of a weed-covered rock, the rushing take of a leviathan to turn the scales at 12lb—and rock fishers' dreams are made of such things!

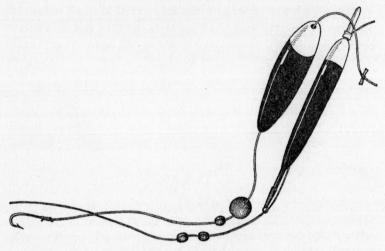

Alternative float rigs for bass. The sliding float and drilled bullet rig, incorporating a length of rubber or thick nylon line as a float stop, is for rough-water use. The fixed float and swan shot is for light fishing in relatively smooth water. In a run of fast water, the larger, sliding float and drilled bullet may make for better tackle control

Sometimes, when one is fishing a fish-bait close to the seabed, a conger eel may take the hook, and then unless one's tackle is exceptionally strong the angler cannot win, for even the comparatively small conger hugs rock with tremendous strength and puts up a fierce, scissoring fight. Fish-baits are essential for the big eels, but a conger rig will rule out all other rock fish and, presented on the bottom, there can be considerable tackle loss.

You do not set out as for normal rock fishing and anticipate conger. You set out to fish for conger, with conger tackle, and philosophically accept that there will be nothing else to enliven the hours between the big eels biting.

In many parts, particularly in the south, mullet hug the coast in large shoals. These shoals may be made up of large fish, and these fish may bring frustration, not at all the fish for the casual angler. Mullet have a reputation of being uncatchable, but this is not strictly true. They are merely very difficult to catch, and consequently seldom caught. They are shy, exceptionally shy, and you will see them in the summer on the surface, and then they will see you, too! If they see you, you will not catch them.

The best mullet tackle is the tackle of the freshwater angler, the long, supple rod, light floats, tiny hooks, and the finest nylon line you can get away with using. Often, in the mullet hot-spots of the Mediterranean, the author has resorted to 2lb b.s. nylon in desperation, and taken fish, but such is fishing to strain the nerves.

You cannot expect to fish a new, unknown venue and take mullet immediately. Doubtless the fish will be there in the summer months, but their presence is not enough. You must know their habits, what they are feeding upon and, having discovered that, you must present the bait in as natural a manner as possible. Exactly what that bait is, is not necessarily of prime importance, but one cannot emphasise too strongly that it must be presented so as to appear to the fish as just another morsel of natural food. You will not be able to achieve this with a clumsy, heavily-shotted float rig.

Perhaps the easiest mullet—and even then *easy* is merely a relative term—are those found in localities where food refuse finds it way into the sea, or alternatively, one may educate the fish to a bait, say bread, but this is a lengthy process. There may be many days, even weeks, to wait before the mullet will take the food you have been introducing at regular intervals, and bread in various forms can be the most convenient bait.

The majority of mullet taken by the author have fallen for a portion of floating crust, presented on a leadless line and cast from a fixed-spool reel. The reel should be loaded to capacity to facilitate smooth and easy casting, the line should be 5lb b.s., and a size 6 freshwater hook is tied direct to this line. There is no other tackle.

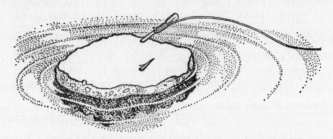

Sections of crust are torn roughly from a loaf, not cut off in neat cubes. The hook is passed through the crust into the white crumb and then brought back through the crust to expose the point

A piece of crust, about one inch across, is put onto the hook and then dunked into the water to give additional casting weight. The angler notes the position of the shoal, and then creeps carefully into position, using whatever cover is available—essentially down off the skyline and preferably without trying to look at the fish after once noting their position. Well back from the waterline, the cast is made with a smooth action, the rod is held almost vertical, and a bight of slack line is pulled off the reel to indicate bites. It is better to cup the hand over the reel to stop further line blowing off the spool, rather than to engage the bail arm, for some bail arms spring back into place with a loud 'clang'. This metallic sound will send the mullet streaking away.

As soon as the line pulls tight, you engage the bail arm of the reel simultaneously with striking in a controlled lift, and start to play the fish immediately. *Play* is the operative word, for mullet are soft-mouthed creatures, and you will not get your fish by heaving and winching. Let the fish run under pressure, then turn it with side strain, let it run again, then turn it again. How often you will have to do this will depend upon the weight of the mullet and the breaking strain of your line, but, whatever happens, do not give the fish a chance to make slack line.

Two things are essential for mullet—fine tackle and caution. Seal this combination with ingenuity, and you *may* catch mullet consistently.

Throughout the summer months your rocks may be visited by shoals of mackerel, and, while these are not truly rock fish, they can provide fast and furious sport on even the brightest afternoon. Here, again, your freshwater tackle has a place, but now sport will be more easily found.

The big shoals of mackerel come close inshore after the shoals of whitebait, and you will have no doubt when they arrive. The water will thrash into foam, so furiously that often you may hear it above the sounds of the sea before you see the commotion.

Side strain, a playing technique which beats a fish in almost half the time taken by conventional, overhead pressure. With side strain you utilise the fish's own power and speed to your benefit as it is turned in the direction of your choice. An essential technique where rocks, weeds, or other snags abound

Mackerel will be seen just below the surface, tearing through the tightly-packed whitebait, breaking the surface in a flurry of water. Then the disturbance ceases and, just as suddenly as they arrived, the mackerel depart.

Your end tackle now is a small Mepps spoon, or a fly spoon, and success depends generally upon your casting ability. The mackerel may range anywhere between 75yd out and the very edge of the rocks, and you must cast quickly and accurately. When you have taken your fish, cast again immediately, for the foraging at the surface is inevitably of short duration.

Keep your tackle down to essentials and travel lightly, for you may find yourself scrambling from rock to rock to get within range of mackerel which have reappeared 60 or 70yd down the shore from their original position. Sometimes, you may feel a fish take the spinner powerfully out on the flank of the mackerel shoal, and the rod will bend over into an alarming arc. You will have hooked a bass, and then your line will break, or you will experience a fight you will never forget.

These are the fish you may expect to encounter in the course of your rock fishing. There may be others, but they will be bonus

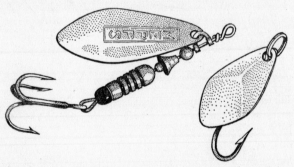

The Mepps spoon, probably the most widely used spinning lure in Europe. The blade revolves in a most attractive manner, even at relatively low speeds. The traditional fly spoon has its devotees also, but while the design makes for attractive movement in the water, the hook does not always provide good purchase

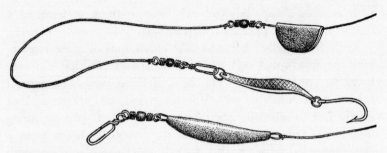

A conventional spinning rig for many species. The lead weight must always be above the swivel to activate the swivel. Fold-over leads, shop-bought or cut from sheet lead, are ideal spinning weights, but one of the best models is the relatively uncommon Wye lead—salmon anglers will know this one! The lure length is attached to the link swivel, the reel line to the static eye

fish. Your fishing season will be during the mild and warm months of the year; from May, reaching a peak in August and September, and extending until the end of November if the weather is kind.

ROCK TACKLE

For the general run of rock fishing, you will need a rod about 10ft long, stiff enough in its action to need a pull of between 1 and 3lb to take it over into a curve, and tubular glass fibre is the ideal material. This is about as close as one may come to a general rod, bearing in mind that there has never been a rod made to cope with all situations and all forms of fishing. If your locale offers good bass fishing, you may care to concentrate on spinning, in which case you must equip yourself with spinning tackle and appreciate that this will not suffice for all forms of rock fishing. If mullet are the quarry, then, you must use the ultra-light tackle which has been mentioned and resign yourself to specialisation. For conger eels, you must again specialise, but to the other extreme, with a powerful rod to strain against a possibly large eel with strong line.

Your reel may be decided by what you have available, for

reels are not cheap, but you will have to think in terms of a
centre-pin or multiplier for conger fishing.

Rock fishing does not normally entail long-distance casting,
and the fixed-spool reel—with spare spools carrying different
breaking strains of line—can be a definite asset. For general
fishing, a spool loaded with 10lb b.s. nylon, and spare spools of
lighter line to allow for special circumstances. If you are going
to buy a fixed spool, ensure that the model is chosen from a
range intended for sea fishing, for salt water can play havoc with
some of the lightweight metals used in the manufacture of freshwater reels. Also, choose a model with the bail arm made of
one piece of stainless steel, as opposed to being made up of several
connections. A solid, one-piece bail arm will be strong enough
to combat some of the occupational hazards of rock fishing, such
as floating rafts of weed—the hauling in of which taxes tackle
to the utmost—washed in constantly to the rocks after a spring
tide.

A selection of all the smaller sizes of sea hooks, a range of
floats—from slim quills to thick, cork-bodied models—a tin of
split shot, some wire traces and lengths of nylon for traces, will
cover much of the fishing. Add a tin of assorted leads—barrel,
drilled bullet, and small lengths of sheet lead—swivels, and
various lures—rubber sand-eels, Mepps, and silver spoons—and

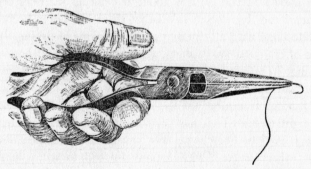

Artery forceps can make good hook removers, but snipe-nosed pliers allow
a better hand grip and have the weight to cope with hard-mouthed species

the rock fisher's tackle box is complete. As essential accessories, one needs a small sharp knife for general work, a pair of snipe-nosed pliers for removing hooks, and a good landing net will be found to be much better than a gaff.

The natural baits of the locale can seldom be bettered, but this obviously entails pre-fishing activity, and rag and lug worm, cuttle, and fish strips, will cover all contingencies.

Travel as lightly as you can, for rock fishing at its best is an exploratory pastime, but do not forget that quite often you may be fishing at the base of sheer cliff or from jagged rocks. Dawn and dusk are normally the most productive times for catching fish on the very edge of the rocks, sometimes regardless of the tide state, but the half light at such times can be dangerous if one is not careful, particularly as dusk sets in.

And here let it be emphasised that while this section of the book embraces rock fishing, it does not set out to cover the tough fishing which takes place on some coasts, the fishing from dangerous perches above wild sea with the tackle settling sometimes as far as 200ft below. Such fishing is not to be recommended in books, but must be left to the decision of the individual as to whether he is prepared to take the very considerable risks involved. And even then he should either be experienced, or in the company of an experienced friend.

In any kind of rock fishing, always watch well how you tread in unknown places and in the excitement of playing a fish, above all, keep aware of the state of the tide. The natural temptation to stay on for 'just one more cast' could result in you being cut off by the sea. Rock fishing is apt to be a comparatively tough form of sea angling, particularly when there are jagged, irregular and slippery rocks to be climbed, but it need not be dangerous—unless you forget that it *can* be!

CHAPTER SEVEN

Angles on Sportfish

THE BALLAN WRASSE *(Labrus bergylta)*

WRASSE are widely distributed throughout the tropical and sub-tropical waters of the world, but few in the many hundreds in this order of fishes are of interest to the angler. The tautog of the Atlantic coast of America, and the scarus of the Mediterranean, are probably top in the sportfish category, for these attain good size and make good eating. The rest of the order are generally small, indifferent fighters, and even poorer table fare. Of the wrasse encountered in European waters, the ballan wrasse is probably the most sought after.

As a whole, wrasse are thickset, heavily-built fish, covered with comparatively large scales which extend onto the gill covers, and the ballan is typical. The leading part of the dorsal fin is

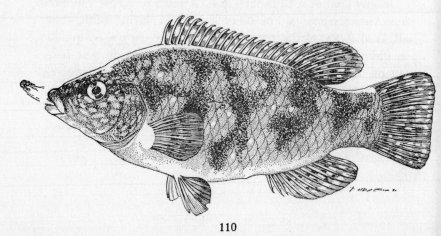

made up of strong spines, and there are three spines to the leading edge of the anal fin. Overall colour varies tremendously with environment and locale, but a fairly typical colouring is olive green on the back, changing to lighter green or blue on the flanks, and merging into buff or orange on the undersides.

The head and flanks in more colourful specimens are often chequered with red or orange, but this is by no means definite and colouring may depend much upon the weeds and rocks in the immediate vicinity, and the mood of the wrasse at the moment.

These fish like rocky, inshore waters, and are well distributed along coastlines which promote rocky outcrops and thick kelp patches. They are particularly prolific on the Irish and West Country coasts.

Wrasse in general seem prone to temperature and pressure changes, and their bodies are often distended when brought up from any appreciable depth. While they are generally caught inshore, the cut traces from deep-water wrecks may well be caused by wrasse, although generally attributed to 'monsters' among the more popular sporting species.

The ballan wrasse has particularly powerful crushing teeth, equal to the task of crushing mussels and small scallops, crabs and crustaceans, and will quite often bite through an angler's line. Generally solitary fish, hugging clefts in a rock face or lurking in thick patches of weed, they may be encountered in dozens around an outcrop which concentrates a food supply. They can provide a tenacious fight when hooked on light, inshore tackle, but are best returned afterwards as they will not provide much of a meal. For this reason, the ballan wrasse has no commercial significance.

THE BASS (*Morone labrax*)

The bass is the only common representative in British waters of the family of sea perches. It is among the greatest of sportfish, and known in some localities as sea wolf, or salmon bass.

Distributed throughout the Mediterranean, ranging west in the Atlantic to Madeira and northwards to the British Isles, the bass is a fish of the warmer waters. Around the British coasts, bass are most common in the south and south-west of England, the south and west coasts of Ireland, and tend to become more thinly distributed the farther north one moves in the North Sea. Bass are relatively uncommon in the north of Scotland, but may be encountered. In 1957, the writer took a superbly conditioned bass of 3lb from 19 fathoms, off Buckie, Banffshire.

The overall colour is silver, the back ranging from dull grey

to olive green, and the flanks showing sheens of blue or green. In some specimens there is a definite bronze sheen to the cheeks and gill covers. These tints fade with death to leave the fish silver to dull grey. The dorsal and caudal fins take the colour of the back, the lower fins being transparent or white. Both the tail and the anal fin have a light marking along the free edges. The first dorsal fin contains between seven and nine sharp spines, the second dorsal has two leading spines followed by between eleven and thirteen soft, branched rays. The pectoral fins are made up of soft rays, without spines. The pelvic fins below each have one spine at the leading edge, and the anal fin has three sharp spines, followed by between ten and twelve soft, branched rays. The spines, in bass of all sizes, are very sharp and can inflict particularly painful wounds. Contrary to belief in some circles, these spines do not inject poison, and any resulting inflamation will be due to neglect of the wound.

Bass range far and wide, in changing environments, for food. They may follow the shoals of whitebait and mackerel, patrol shingle banks for small flatfish, or come right inshore into very shallow water for sand-eels, sand-hoppers, shrimps, and crabs. Thus there is contrast in the fishing, with such extremes as Ireland's famous Splaugh Rock or the comparatively quiet, brackish water of a river mouth, and the difference in the venue calls for a corresponding difference in fishing technique. Bass are fiercely predatory, but the large fish can be subtle in their feeding habits.

A rod-caught record bass of 18lb 2oz was taken at Felixstowe in 1943, and various authorities have noted fish around the 20lb mark, but these are huge fish. Sportfish range between 2 and 6lb, and larger bass are in the big-fish class. Those exceeding 10lb are exceptional fish, and are, unfortunately, few and far between. Whatever the size, the bass, on suitable tackle, is renowned as a tenacious fighting fish.

THE BLACK BREAM (*Spondyliosoma cantharus*)

This sea bream is one of the two species visiting European coasts in sufficient numbers to be truly considered a sportfish. Dis-

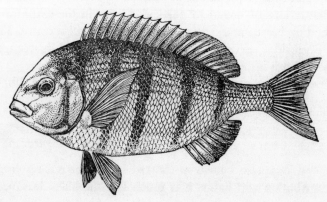

tributed widely throughout the Mediterranean and the adjacent Atlantic, these bream come inshore in large shoals during the spring and early summer and are then to be found in deep, fast water over rocky ground. As the summer progresses, the large shoals disperse, the fish becoming spread over much wider areas but still favouring the faster water over rocks.

The overall colour of the black bream is deep blackish blue or purple on the back, fading to sliver on the flanks and belly and sometimes shot with a pink tinge. The long, spined dorsal fin normally takes the colour of the back, with the remaining fins dull grey, other than the tail fin, which is yellowish grey. Quite often, there are suggestions of black vertical bands on the upper flank, and brown horizontal stripes below the lateral line. There is no shoulder patch.

All manner of marine worms and crustaceans, and probably small fish, are taken by bream, and the jaws and very powerful teeth suggest that they have no trouble in crushing various shellfish. Black bream shelter from strong currents in the lee of rocks, taking whatever food is available there, but dashing out into the fast water whenever another food form is presented by the tide.

Tenacious fighters when hooked on light tackle, these bream attract thousands of anglers annually out to the deep-water, rocky marks. It is probable that spawning activity attracts great concentrations of bream to particular spots in the sea, and two of the best bream marks are to be found off British coasts. These are Bembridge Ledge, in the Solent, and off Littlehampton, Sussex, and it is debatable which is the better of the two.

The size of shoaling black bream is between 1 and 3lb, but the species probably attains weights above 6lb.

THE COMMON SEA BREAM (*Pagellus bogaraveo*)

This species is also known as the red bream, or red sea bream. In distribution and habits it is much like the black bream, but appears to be rather more spasmodic in its movements. It will establish itself in certain areas each summer for years, and then the stocks will wane or disappear for no apparent reason. The fish may never appear again in one of these areas, or they may return in their original strength after a number of years have passed. This pattern of behaviour has been noted particularly in Irish waters, and also off the west coast of England.

While the basic shape of black bream and red bream is almost identical, there is no room for confusion for, as the name implies, the red bream is overall coloured dull red, fading to silvery pink on the flanks. The fins are red or orange-red, and the pectoral fins are long and sweeping; considerably longer than those of the black bream. There is a distinct black patch on the shoulder at the origin of the lateral line.

Red bream, while encountered at all levels, are generally found nearer the bottom and closer inshore than black bream, but the inshore fish are normally quite small fish, the sizes increasing progressively the farther one moves out into deep water.

The average weight for these deep-water shoal bream may be 2 to 5lb, with occasional four- or five-pounders. A red bream of over 7lb has been recorded from Fowey, Cornwall, and the Irish record fish committee recognises a red bream of over 9lb, caught off Valentia Island in 1963.

THE COD (*Gadus morhua*)

In recent years with the great swing towards sea angling, the cod has become one of the most important of sportfish. Found on both sides of the Atlantic, it is abundant in the northern North Sea and Scottish waters, but the greatest concentrations are encountered off Norway and Iceland. While cod may be found throughout the year at many southern deep-water marks, it is in winter that the large shoals normally move inshore. The winters of 1967 and 1968 brought huge concentrations of cod to British south coast points, and the Kent coast—in particular, marks off Newhaven—was regularly the scene of large catches of fish, with specimens up to 35lb.

The overall colour of cod is somewhat variable, depending upon environment, and ranges from greyish-yellow to dull grey for fish over sand and mud, to reddish-brown for fish caught over heavily-weeded or rocky ground. The body is profusely marked with spots which are often golden-brown or greenish-brown, cod from rockly locales tending to have much darker

spot markings. The lateral line is broad and white, sloping down behind the pectorals and defined by concentrations of the body spots along both sides. Fins are normally a darker shade of the body colour, without spot markings.

The head is large, the shoulders and belly substantial, but tapering off abruptly to the tail regions. The snout protrudes beyond the upper, longer jaw, and the large thick-lipped mouth is well armed with sharp teeth. There is a distinctive barbel below the chin.

Cod are shoal fish, predominantly ground-feeders, but rising in the water to take whatever food is available. They are particularly voracious feeders with seemingly insatiable appetites, and most forms of marine life are preyed upon at one time or another. Cuttle, squid, star-fish, rocklings, dragonets, and dabs, and even whelks, crabs, and small lobsters, are standard fare, while herring and mackerel are taken as they become available.

Thousands of very large cod must come inshore each year, for fish of 30lb, or more, are caught fairly consistently on rod and line in European waters, and several in excess of 40lb have been taken in British waters in recent years. The world record cod, taken off Brielle, New Jersey, in 1967, weighed 81lb. However, huge cod, more than double the size of the average rod-caught fish, are often taken by commercial fishermen, and the author has examined several around the 50lb mark taken in nets off Iceland. Many larger have been recorded, but still these are small fry in comparison with a leviathan of 211lb, said to have been taken off Massachusetts, USA, by a trawler in 1895.

THE CONGER EEL (*Conger conger*)

The conger eel is widely distributed in European seas, extending northwards to Scandinavian waters. It is commonly encountered in Irish waters and in the Channel, and perhaps the greatest concentration is to be found off the west coast of the British Isles.

Unless one considers the common eel—*Anguilla anguilla*—there is nothing with which to confuse the conger. The conger grows big, very big, and the body is thick and muscular. The head is broad, the eye large, and the mouth, extending beyond the line of the eye, is armed with sharp, closely-set teeth. The scaleless body is covered with a thick slime, and overall colour varies from dull pinkish-brown to purple-grey, fading to off-white or light grey on the belly.

Conger normally reside in rocks and other seabed obstructions from the very edge of the sea, sometimes left exposed at low water, to depths in excess of 100 fathoms. Harbour walls and pier supports invariably have cracks and crevices which hold relatively large conger. Such eels would be almost totally nocturnal in their foraging abroad for food, but they can be encountered in deep water during all hours of the day. In the normal course of events, where light penetrates the water to any great extent congers will stay in their lairs until nightfall, then slide

out to quest for food in the open, sometimes even swimming to the surface in warm weather. Extremely susceptible to cold, large specimens are occasionally washed ashore in winter in a stupor, or dead, and I saw dozens of eels dying in the Solent when the inshore waters froze during the terrible winter of 1962–3.

Conger are essentially predators, taking all manner of creatures encountered during their quest for food. Smaller conger, all types of bottom-dwelling fish, crabs, shellfish, cuttles, squid, and marine worms are all taken readily.

When in trouble, the conger tends to back away from whatever threatens it, doubling up upon itself and using its tail to grip the smallest obstruction to advantage. The conger moves into breaks in the rocks tail-first, and even on dry land it is the tail which thrusts and clamps to support the movement of the rest of the body. Unlike a normal fight, where one decides the issue by being able to turn a fish's head, one now has to overcome the power of the conger's tail, which could be lapped in a crack, or wrapped about a spar, with tremendous holding power.

The British record conger of 84lb, from Dungeness, reigned unchallenged for thirty-seven years, but in June 1970, international sea angler, Colin Chapman, fishing out of Brixham, Devon, caught a huge eel weighing 85 lb. Are there bigger eels? The *Illustrated London News* for 17 September, 1904, carried an illustration of a conger eel which was 9ft long and weighed 160lb!

THE COMMON SKATE *(Raja batis)*

This ray is widely and generously distributed throughout Europe and found at varying depths around the British Isles. Sand and shingle, and rough bottoms of a relatively flat nature attract this

fish, and over such ground it is commonly encountered from inshore to deep-water marks in excess of 100 fathoms.

The top colour of the common skate shows considerable variation, ranging through dark brown and grey, with darker patches, and it is sometimes very attractively marked with a profusion of spots and a large dark marking in the centre of each wing. The underside is never pure white, rather a streaky buff or grey, with sometimes the grey streaking concentrating into a very dark patch in the centre of the belly.

Food consists of all manner of crustaceans and shellfish, and small fish, but particularly tiny skate and flatfishes; the big skate flopping over them and engulfing them on the seabed.

The top weight for this species is said to be 400lb, and this is quite feasible. Certainly, they regularly reach weights in excess of 200lb. A rod-caught skate off Ballycotton, in 1913—which somehow did not feature in the record list—weighed 221lb. Another, from the Isle of Man, in 1925, weighed 200lb, and the current British record fish, from the Orkneys, in 1968, weighed 214lb.

THE THORNBACK *(Raja clavata)*

This ray is widely distributed in European seas, found quite commonly in the Mediterranean, and is plentiful around the British Isles. Possibly the biggest concentration of thornbacks is to be found in the Irish Sea.

The thornback is the ray most commonly seen by anglers, often very small, but regularly caught in considerable numbers. The immediate identification is found in the spines or thorns from which the ray takes its name, and which are situated in the centre regions of the wings and along the body. While most other species have a number of spines, mainly along the back and on the tail, the thornback is the only commonly found ray with spines centred on the wings. Another ray, *Raja radiata*, has even larger spines in the centre of the wings, but this species is comparatively rare.

Overall colour is variable, generally a shade of brown but also ranging to grey, and normally marked with a profusion of spots, often forming very attractive patterns. The spots may range from near-white through four or five shades of the background colour

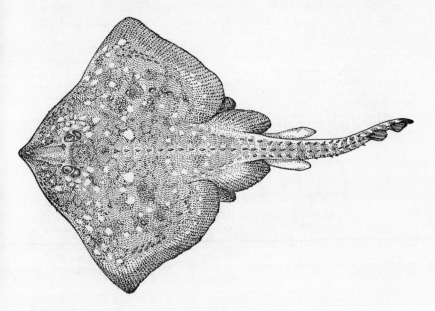

to dark brown. The underside is sharply white in contrast.

Although the rod-caught record is held by a ray of 38lb, from Rustington Beach in 1935, a ten-pounder is a very good fish. The largest the author has seen weighed is 16lb, but between 4 and 8lb is a fairly standard weight.

THE FLOUNDER *(Platichthys flesus)*

The flounder, fluke, or white fluke, as it is variously known, is widely spread and abundant in the Mediterranean, the adjacent

Atlantic, and around the British Isles, extending northwards in its range to Iceland.

This fish is relatively thick in the body, rather angular in appearance, and has a larger mouth than the plaice. The main body is fairly smooth to the touch, but rough scales are concentrated behind the eyes and over the pectoral fin, and a line of rough scales follows the lines of the main fins. These scales are absent in the plaice. The overall colour ranges from dull grey

to dark greenish-brown, with light marblings or dark patches, and occasionally pale orange spots. Overall colour is dependent upon the nature and colour of the seabed, with body colouring changing in seconds to match a different environment, and, for this reason, several flounders from the same locale may show wide variance.

A shallow-water species, the flounder is found over mud, clay, sand and shingle banks. Predominantly a fish of harbours and estuaries, flounders often penetrate many miles into fresh water. They feed mainly upon crustaceans, marine worms, and tiny, bottom-dwelling fish.

A 2lb flounder is a first-class fish on light tackle, and anything above that weight is exceptional. While fish above 3lb are rarely encountered, the British record stands at 5lb 11oz.

THE HADDOCK *(Melanogrammus aeglifinus)*

This fish is widely distributed on both sides of the Atlantic but is most abundant in European waters, perhaps having its greatest concentration off Iceland, and then in the northern North Sea.

Elsewhere in European waters, haddock have suffered tremendously from the effects of over-fishing by commercial fishermen, but there are occasional good years when haddock seem to be present in large numbers off Scottish and Irish coasts.

Very similar in shape to the cod, the haddock is identified immediately by its distinctive, black shoulder marks, and the lack of the cod's overall spot markings. Overall colour is grey to dull olive fading over the flanks, these shot with bronze and silver sheens. Fins are generally dull brown, and the first dorsal is high and angular. The tail-fin is gently forked.

Haddock are normally medium- and deep-water fish and appear to feed upon smaller fish to a lesser extent than similar species in the deep-water environment. Food seems to consist predominantly of crustaceans, in the form of shrimps, hermit crabs, and Norway lobsters, but star-fish, shellfish, cuttles, and marine worms also make up the staple diet. Haddock are in their best condition during the winter months, when they forage inshore before migrating out to deep water to spawn in the spring.

While average haddock might weigh around 4lb, the author has seen a brace of seven-pounders taken in a trawl off Iceland in 1959. Early authorities refer to a haddock of over 24lb from Dublin Bay, but it is strange that there are no other records of haddock coming anywhere near to the weight of that giant. However, one cannot discount it on those grounds. Among outstanding rod-caught haddock of comparatively recent years are a fish from Bridlington, in 1962, weighing 7lb 15 oz, and one from Kinsale, in 1964, which weighed 10lb 13 oz.

THE HAKE *(Merluccius merluccius)*

The hake is found in the Mediterranean, in the Bay of Biscay and along the deep-water marks off Spain and Portugal, but is perhaps most abundant in the deep northern waters of the North Sea; a truly oceanic fish of the deep, remoter parts. Norwegian and Irish waters hold sizeable hake, but even then the fish are not common, for they are slow-growing and intensive commercial fishing over the years has taken its toll.

In general shape, the hake resembles the ling—*Molva molva*— but the head and shoulders of the hake are more substantial and the tapering of the body away to the tail more obvious. The head is broad, the mouth coloured black inside and armed with long, sharp teeth. The lower jaw tends to protrude and there is no barbel. The number and positions of the fins are exactly as on the ling, but the hake's fins are made up of harder rays and the leading dorsal is more angular.

The overall colour is silver grey, dark on the back and often infused with browns, and sometimes the suggestion of dark spots. The colour lightens on the lower flanks and belly, but generally the main impression is of a dark grey fish. The lateral line is black, and virtually straight from gill cover to tail.

A voracious fish-eater, the hake will take whatever is available in fish, often its own kind, but depending upon environment. Whiting and Norway pout, and smaller hake, are probably staple

diet, but herring, mackerel and pilchards augment this when the hake moves into shallower water.

Fish-baits are the obvious requirement, but the rewards for an angler bent solely on hake would be poor indeed. Most rod-caught hake comes as a surprise bonus to anglers fishing deep-water marks for other species.

THE HALIBUT *(Hippoglossus hippoglossus)*

This is the giant of the flatfishes, the leviathan of dark, cold, and often dangerous waters. Perhaps the greatest concentration of these fish is to be found off Newfoundland, with the range extending from the American coast to Iceland, and then thinning down

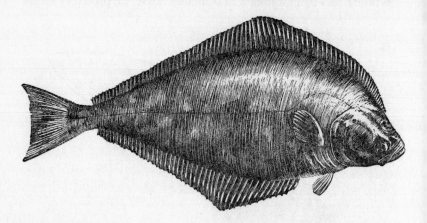

through Norwegian waters to a southern limit on the European side in the Channel. Predominantly, it is a fish of Arctic waters, with the halibut around the British Isles restricted to the Shetlands and Faroes, northern Scotland, the northern part of the North Sea, and Ireland.

In recent years, anglers have sought halibut in deep, rugged water off Scotland, and angling festivals have grown on the strength of the publicity given to this in the angling press, but really the rod-caught specimens are tiny fish when one considers the size potential of the species. As they are truly deep-water fish, known to inhabit depths of up to 500 fathoms, one can only speculate upon the size a really huge halibut might reach in the security of the dark rock gullies, but commercial fishermen have landed hundreds in excess of 200lb, mainly from the Grand

Banks. The largest ever recorded (Cape Ann, Gulf of Maine, 1917) was reputed to weigh, after cleaning at the Boston fish pier, between 615 and 625lb. J. Travis Jenkins in *Fishes of the British Isles* mentions a halibut of 320lb from off the Isle of Man, but more recently, although I can find no definite reference to hand, the national press gave considerable coverage in the 1950s to a halibut of over 500lb brought into Grimsby.

The halibut is narrower than the conventional flatfish shape, and very thick in the body. Overall colour is uniformly dark, sometimes almost black, but generally ranging from olive green to slate brown. The smaller fish tend to have mottled patterns, and the underside is pearl white. The scales are almost unnaturally smooth for such a large flatfish, and the lateral line curves down sharply behind the pectoral fin. The mouth is large, and armed with very sharp teeth.

A predator, the halibut will take all manner of fish, crustaceans and molluscs, but standard foods seem to be haddock, whiting, sole, dabs, Norway lobsters, and squids.

Few anglers indeed, in Europe, would attempt to give advice on halibut sportfishing, but doubtless, in time, the fascination of rugged conditions and a huge adversary will produce specialists in the pastime. Certainly one would need exceptionally strong, specialised tackle to fish large fish-baits in what could be treacherous waters. From what I have been able to gather, the average halibut moves off with a bait in what seems to be an almost unstoppable run—and the really big ones have yet to be contacted!

THE LING *(Molva molva)*

The ling is a creature of the deeps, a predator of rock formations, reefs, and wrecks, sometimes encountered over shingle or mud but mainly where the seabed provides contrast for its almost eel-like way of life.

It is found widely in the deeps of the North Atlantic and all around the British coasts where the water is deep over rocks, but the most famous mark to come to light in recent years is without doubt the wreck of the *Lusitania*, off the Old Head of Kinsale, in Ireland.

The ling is not a true shoal fish, but conditions at the bottom of the sea may serve to congregate many fish in a comparatively small area—for example, concentrations of food around and in a wreck, or rock formation—and thus, once contact has been made, ling may be encountered in good numbers.

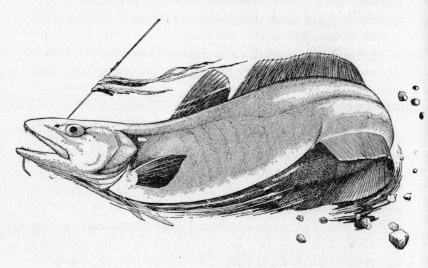

The overall colour varies through olive and brown to grey, becoming lighter on the lower flanks and sometimes mottled with dark markings. The dorsal, tail and anal fins have a white piping to the free edge, and the chin bears a distinctive barbel. These are points which identify it immediately from the hake, which is basically similar in appearance but does not attain the same size.

Just how large ling do grow is very much a matter for speculation, for comparatively little is known about them. The nature of their environment restricts study somewhat, and it is only in comparatively recent years that sizeable fish have come to light in any numbers. A similar situation exists with conger eels, and provides a parallel.

Travis Jenkins, in *Fishes of the British Isles* (1925), gives the usual length as 'from four to six feet, but it sometimes attains a length of seven feet', and Couch has recorded a ling of 124lb from a mark off the Scilly Isles. There seems no reason to doubt the authenticity of the 45lb fish from Penzance, in 1912, but talk of ling weighing between 60 and 70lb caught in the Gulf of Mexico only adds confusion, for 'ling' is a local name for the cobia—*Rachycentron canadus*.

Ling are almost certainly exclusively fish-eaters. They may also feed upon crustaceans and cuttle, but the main fare is flat-fishes and other bottom fish : gurnard, scad, dragonets, and small conger.

THE MACKEREL *(Scomber scombrus)*

The mackerel is found in the Mediterranean, and from Gibraltar to Norway. A nomadic fish, it is not connected with any par-ticular type of sea environment, but shoals near the surface of

I

the sea and moves inshore during the spring and summer months to harry the shoals of whitebait. As the winter approaches, the shoals move out to sea and travel deep, some to winter on the edge of the continental shelf. In the summer, starting in June and ending, if the weather is good, in October, mackerel come right inshore around the British Isles, following the shoals of whitebait and motivated purely by the presence of the fry.

There is no mistaking the mackerel in European waters. The streamlined but substantial body tapers sharply off to the tail section, with its series of little finlets and scythe-like tail, and there is the metallic blue-green of the back and upper flanks, broken by the distinctive black bar markings. In all ways it is an excellent fish : in appearance, for sport, and for eating.

The inshore shoals tend to travel in company with fish of much the same length and weight, probably with a top weight of 1½lb. The larger mackerel are invariably encountered out over deep waters by boat anglers, and it is among these fish, even on the bottom at the beginning or tail-end of the season, that one stands best chance of contacting the 2½- or 3-pounders. Since 1952, the record has crept steadily up over the 4lb mark, with the largest fish to date being a 5lb 6½oz specimen from off the Eddystone Light in 1969.

THE GREY MULLET

Three species of grey mullet from the many types present in warm and temperate seas will interest the European angler. These three will appear so similar to each other that, in common with most anglers, he will probably think of them only as grey mullet and ignore the characteristics distinguishing the different species. However, the thick-lipped grey mullet—*Crenimugil labrosus*—the thin-lipped grey mullet—*Chelon ramada*—and the golden grey mullet—*Chelon auratus*—may be encountered in salt, fresh, or brackish waters on the European side of the Atlantic, with the range extending northwards as far as Bergen in Norway.

Basically, the grey mullets are all much of a muchness, stream-lined but substantially built, the back blue-grey fading to silver-grey on the flanks and white on the belly, with the back and flanks marked horizontally with dark grey bars from nose to tail. The mouth is small, with tiny, weak teeth, and the eye is set well forward on the head. The leading dorsal fin is supported by four hard spines, the pectoral fins are placed high on the body, and no lateral line is present. The simplest method of identifying the three mentioned species is to note the difference in distance between the first and second dorsal fins. There are other features, but the fins provide the most easily remembered pointers.

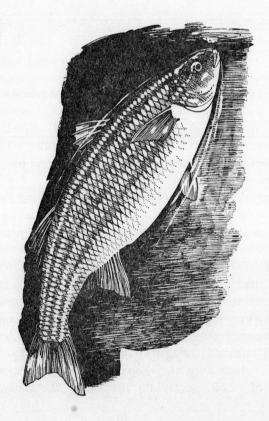

The base length of the first dorsal fin, horizontally, when the fin is opened, is used as a measure. In the thin-lipped grey mullet, the second dorsal is placed twice the length of the first dorsal fin behind. In the golden grey mullet, one and a half times behind, and in the thick-lipped grey mullet, almost exactly the same length as the first dorsal fin behind. A further aid to distinguish between thick-lipped and thin-lipped grey mullet is found underneath the head in the shape of the gill covers meeting under the chin; known as the jugular interspace. In thick-lipped mullet,

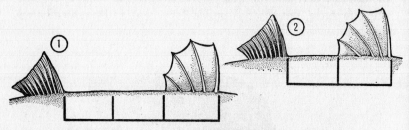

(1) Thin-lipped grey mullet. (2) Thick-lipped grey mullet

the edges of the gill covers run almost parallel, while in the thin-lipped mullet they curve away from each other. The golden grey mullet has a distinctive and well-defined gold patch on each gill cover.

Able to adapt themselves to a range of environments from the salt water of the open coastline, through the brackish water of estuaries and pure fresh water of rivers, to the near-stagnant waters of marsh pools, the grey mullets are shy, subtle fish, moving in shoals of just two or three fish to perhaps three or four hundred, and often seemingly unattainable to the angler.

In a natural, unaffected environment, mullet feed upon minute insects, larvae, plant detritus absorbed from mud and gravel, and filamentous algae scoured off rocks, pilings, and boats' hulls. Such fish invariably bring nothing but frustration to the angler. However, where ships and shoreside dwellings promote regular deposits of edible waste into the water, the mullet become educated to such easy pickings as bread and other mainly floating forms of food, and then they offer the angler a better chance. Even then the tackle should be very fine and the angler cautious in his approach.

Thick-lipped and thin-lipped grey mullets grow well into double figures and, while a near-17lb fish is on record as having been netted from Pagham harbour, the largest rod-caught mullet from British waters weighed just over 10lb and was taken at Portland in 1952.

In the author's experience, the South Mole at Gibraltar offers the best grey mullet fishing available anywhere. There, 4, 5, and 6lb mullet were often taken, and 'uncatchable' fish of perhaps 8 or 10lb were sometimes seen.

THE PLAICE *(Pleuronectes platessa)*

This flatfish ranges from the Mediterranean, occasionally entering the Baltic Sea, and extending northwards in its range to Iceland. Distributed widely around the British Isles, heavy local populations exist in parts of the North Sea, Irish Sea, and the Channel,

generally off steeply shelving shores with shingle grounds offering shellfish and crustaceans.

Plaice grow larger than flounders, are less angular in appearance, fairly smooth to the touch, and are attractively coloured as flatfish go. The overall colour ranges through shades of brown, sometimes having an olive tint, and contrast is provided in large red or orange spots, these spots being sometimes encircled with white in large specimens.

The smaller fish are located very close inshore during the summer months, over sand and marl, where small cockles and razor-fish are to be found and where the nature of the bottom allows the fish to bury themselves. The larger fish are invariably found well out in the deeper water.

A plaice of 3lb is a good fish, and above that weight exceptional, but it is feasible to believe that the species reaches 10lb or more. The British record rod-caught plaice weighed 7lb 15oz, and was caught at Salcombe in 1964, and a fish caught off Portrush, in Ireland, the same year, weighed 7lb.

THE POLLACK *(Pollachius pollachius)*

A fish of rugged seabed and rock formations, pollack seem limited in their distribution to the western coasts of Europe, from Iceland to Norway, through to the Mediterranean. They seem particularly generously distributed around the British Isles but, while fairly plentiful, tend to be far outnumbered by coalfish in Scottish waters. Coalfish seem to become more abundant the farther one moves north.

The fish the Americans call 'pollack' may be encountered along the length of the North American continent, particularly in the Gulf of Maine and off Nova Scotia, but this is in fact the coalfish *(Pollachius virens)*. Strangely, some American writers insist that pollack are known as coalfish, or green cod, in Europe.

Most authorities classified the pollack in with cod at one time, and the fish was then known as *Gadus pollachius*. This was the case until the early 1960s, but *Pollachius pollachius* is now generally accepted for the pollack.

Pollack seem to change their overall colour according to environment and locale, ranging from brown on the back fading to olive on the flanks, to shades of green or grey and the flanks mottled with line markings, particularly in the smaller fish.

There is no barbel on the lower jaw, the eye is large, the lateral line curved, and the tail squared-off, rather than forked, in mature fish. The pelvic fins seem abnormally small, and are conventional fins as opposed to the filaments present in the cods.

The fish most likely to be confused with pollack are undoubtably coalfish. Both are very much alike, but the coalfish is rounder in the body and the head is broader. The lateral line of the coalfish is white and virtually straight, while that of the pollack curves down behind the pectoral. The tiny barbel on the lower jaw of the coalfish is absent in the pollack.

Pollack may be encountered over sand or mud in sheltered water, but such an encounter is merely one of the vagaries of fish movements. A fish which ranges through all levels of water, it is invariably found in the vicinity of rock formations, the larger fish coming from remote parts. Without doubt, Ireland provides some of the best fishing venues for this species in Europe, with Devon and Cornwall coming a close second. While an authenticated $23\frac{1}{2}$-pounder was taken on rod and line off Newquay, Cornwall, in 1957, near 30-pounders have been taken in nets off Ireland. Average weights, however, seem to vary between 2 and 7lb at most marks.

A voracious feeder, the pollack eats all manner of worms and crustaceans, and preys upon sprats, sand-eels, pilchards and herring as these become available. They are active inshore during spring and summer months, but move out to deeper water as the winter sets in.

THE BLUE SHARK *(Carcharinus glauca)*

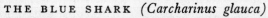
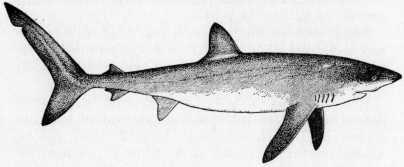

This shark is to be found throughout the world in tropical and temperate seas, ranging through Europe at the influence of the North Atlantic Drift, and appearing off British coasts generally in June and July. Predominantly a shark of deep water, the blue shark will feed at all levels, and is occasionally sighted on the surface in very warm weather.

The blue is a long, slim-bodied species with relatively small fins except for the pectorals, which appear comparatively long. The upper lobe of the tail is very long and distinctly notched. Overall colour is blue, often an intensely vivid blue over the back, dulling and fading on the flanks to white on the belly. The gill-slits are very small by comparison with those of the porbeagle.

Mackerel, pilchards, and herrings are the main quarry of the blue shark, but it will take all manner of fish and other creatures.

Blue shark do not run very large in British waters, or, rather, are not contacted by anglers. Average fish tend to range from 50 to 75lb, with those topping 100lb considered large. The British record blue shark weighed 218lb, from Looe in Cornwall in 1959, and an Irish shark, from Achill, Co. Mayo, in the same year, weighed 206lb. These, however, fall short of the world record caught the following year off Rockport, Mass., a fine shark of 410lb.

THE MAKO *(Isurus oxyrinchus)*

This shark is predominantly a shark of tropical waters, considered a big-game fish even in the true big-game waters of the world, and while it will not tolerate cold waters, it is encountered in Europe to some extent, particularly off parts of the British Isles during the warmer months of the year.

Similar in shape to the porbeagle, the mako is somewhat slimmer, but is still more heavily built than the blue shark. The immediate point of identification is the tail, both lobes being virtually the same size and giving a much more symmetrical appearance than is found in the tails of other sharks likely to be encountered in European waters. There is a long lateral keel on each side of the tail section, but no secondary keel on the lower lobe, as in the porbeagle. Overall colour ranges from dull blue to purple-grey, but this colour is never as vivid as that of the blue shark.

Discovered in British waters only during recent years, and quite often believed to be porbeagles, the great majority of mako shark have come from Cornish waters, although one of 174lb was landed at Kinsale in the 1960s. The one-time British record mako came from Falmouth, in 1964, and weighed 476lb, but

this was superseded in 1966 by a 498lb mako from off Looe. The shark accepted by the International Game Fish Association as a world record weighed 1,000lb, and was taken off Mayor Island, New Zealand, in 1943.

THE PORBEAGLE (*Lamna nasus*)

This shark is widely distributed in the temperate waters of the North Atlantic, but the full distribution and range have never been pin-pointed with any accuracy, and it is probable that un-suspected porbeagle are to be encountered at many points around the British Isles. Certainly they occur in considerable numbers off the west coast of Ireland, in the North Sea, and the Bristol Channel and, while the Co. Clare coast, and Looe, Cornwall, have been well-known porbeagle venues for some time, the Solent has very recently sprung into prominence with large catches of porbeagle. Indeed, one of these shark, a 324-pounder from off the Isle of Wight, held the British record during 1968.

Deeper in the body than any other of the British sharks, the porbeagle has a comparatively large eye, very large gill-slits, and the leading edge of the dorsal fin starts immediately over the rear of the pectoral fin. The upper lobe of the tail is large, and an essential point of identification is found in the two lateral keels on the tail. Overall colour is grey-blue, or grey-brown, fading over the flanks to white on the belly.

Following a line of impressively large fish—311lb, Looe, 1961,

324lb, Solent, 1968, 365lb, Achill, 1932—caught in British waters, a porbeagle of 430lb, caught off Guernsey in 1969, established a new world record for the species.

THE THRESHER SHARK *(Alopias vulpinus)*

Also known as the fox shark, the thresher is distributed widely throughout the warmer waters of the world and is quite common in European seas. Regular seasonal visitors to the Irish coasts and to the south-west of England, these sharks are often seen, but seldom caught by anglers.

There is no reason to confuse any of the sharks normally encountered in British waters with the thresher, for its extraordinary long tail, almost half the length of the body, identifies it immediately.

Very active in the surface regions, thresher are generally seen attacking shoals of mackerel and herrings, and it is popularly assumed—although the author has yet to meet anyone who has actually witnessed it—that the long tail is used for harrying the mackerel and driving them into a tight pack.

While thresher sharks, compared with mako and porbeagle, have long been noted and tried for off British coasts, very few have actually been caught. The British record has stood since 1933 with a fish of 280lb taken off Dungeness, but this is a small shark in comparison to the world record of 922lb, taken in the Bay of Islands, New Zealand, in 1937.

THE SPUR-DOG *(Squalus acanthias)*

Known in some parts as spiny-dog, or piked dogfish, this fish is widely distributed throughout the temperate seas of the world, but is not found in tropical waters. It is common throughout Europe and particularly around the British Isles.

The overall colour of spur-dogs varies from dull brown, through brown-grey, to purplish-grey, occasionally with light spot markings on the back and upper flanks. A slim-bodied species, it can immediately be identified by the bone-like spines on the leading edges of the dorsal fins. These spines are extremely strong, rigid and sharp, and the thrusting of a spur-dog with spines erect and bristling could inflict a deep wound on the unwary angler.

Spur-dogs are encountered in shoals, which could be made up of anything from twenty or thirty fish to literally thousands. Such a shoal would work its way through the sea at all levels, the spur-dog above taking mackerel, herrings, or whatever fish were available, and those below taking gurnards and flatfishes. With

the activity caused by the feeding of such a large shoal on the move, it is improbable that even larger fish, fairly immune from the dogfish, would stay in the vicinity. These large marauding shoals are not normally welcomed in an area by anglers, for then all other sport ceases.

Spur-dogs weighing 10lb and more are not too uncommon, and several fish over 16lb have challenged for the record in recent years, upping the weight a few ounces at a time.

THE TOPE (*Galeorhinus galeus*)

'Blue Dog', 'Toper', even 'Sweet William', they call the tope in some parts of Britain. 'Lagger', 'Hound-fish', and 'Soup-fin shark'

it is called in other parts of the world. In the Straits off Malaya, the Chinese seek the tope for its fins, for this is the shark of the famous shark's-fin soup. In British fish shops the tope is tallied as 'Dutch eel' or 'Rock Cod'—Billingsgate Market jargon to make these unattractive-looking fishes commercially acceptable.

The tope is a comparatively small, slim-bodied shark which ranges throughout the waters of the world. In European waters it moves inshore during the warmer months, from May until October, sometimes coming very close inshore over shingle or sandy beaches. The overall colour is blue-grey or dull brown, fading over the flanks to white on the belly. While the general run of tope weigh between 25 and 40lb, the largest British rod-caught tope weighed 74lb, and was caught off Caldy Island in 1964. Prior to this, a 73-pounder from Hayling Island held the record for fifteen years. Some areas around the British Isles are noted for a run of larger-than-average tope, and the best of these are The Wash, the Thames Estuary—off Herne Bay—the Solent—off Hayling and the Needles—Donegal and Sligo.

Tope feed mainly upon fish, chiefly the free-swimming types in deep water but also flatfishes when foraging inshore.

THE WHITING *(Merlangius merlangus)*

The whiting is a slender, streamlined fish, basically similar in shape to the cod, but the head is longer and more finely built. The upper jaw protudes beyond the lower jaw, and both are armed with comparatively long, sharp teeth. The tail-fin is

squared off, and there is a conspicuous black mark at the point
where the pectoral fins join the body. The eye is relatively large,
and sensory pits are very obvious on the head and gill covers.
Overall colour is dull silver, the back colour varying from bronze
to light brown and merging to silver on the flanks, these sometimes being finely mottled with broken lines and spots of pale
brown or mauve. The dark lateral line is narrow, unlike that
of the cod, and slopes down behind the pectoral fin. The pelvic
fins are long and sinuous, unlike the short fins of the pollack, and
a fine white marking extends the length of the free edges of the
anal and dorsal fins.

Although extending to Iceland in their distribution, whiting
are predominantly southern in range and are most commonly
encountered to the south and west of Ireland, in the Channel and
the North Sea. Found in big shoals at all levels, the fish are in
prime condition during the winter months.

Whiting feed mainly upon smaller fish—their own kind, herrings, sprats and sand-eels—but will also take marine worms and
crustaceans. Good average whiting would weigh around 2lb, but
a fish taken from Loch Shieldaig in 1940 weighed 6lb.

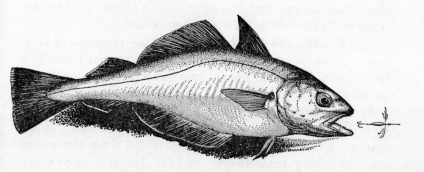

CHAPTER EIGHT

Some essential Knots and Hitches

AMONG the dozens of knots and variations of knots, some are hang-overs from the days of linen lines and while they were no doubt very good in their time, the advent of nylon monofilament has now rendered manv of them obsolete. Monofilament is relatively hard and very smooth, tends to stretch and slide, and completely lacks the coarse, gripping surface of the old woven lines.

A good knot for nylon must rule out any risk of connecting parts sliding upon themselves, and be so constructed as to enable the line to form a purchase upon itself despite the smoothness of its surface. And so the angler must consider the properties of nylon itself when thinking in terms of knots—and this quite apart from the fact that, whichever knot is chosen, the breaking strain of the line will be lowered to some extent.

One should try to assemble tackle with the minimum of knots and concentrate upon learning to tie only essential knots. It is far better to be able to tie one knot securely than to make half a dozen indifferent ones.

With variations on a common whipping, and two or three other knots, the angler should be equipped efficiently for all manner of rigs. Whipping, in my experience, is superior to any knot for joining hooks to line, and certainly does not weaken the line to the same extent as a knot. I make a point of painting a whipping with clear nail varnish once the whipping has been drawn tight, and this dries extremely quickly and ensures a good purchase.

One of the most versatile of knots is that known as the 'double loop', 'double figure-of-eight', or 'blood bight' knot. This can be used in many rigs, from joining lengths of line to forming loops for a paternoster, and is ideal for trace loops, even in wire. I have never known this knot, tied securely, to show any fault in holding.

For attaching line to swivels, or other eyed items of tackle, the 'half-blood' knot is a well-tried favourite, but I like to paint this over, too, with nail varnish to be on the safe side.

Whipping a line to the shank of the hook can be a tiresome procedure, particularly in bad weather, but I believe a whipping

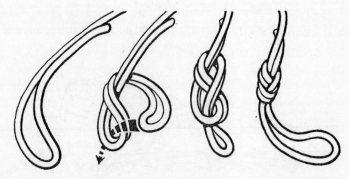

The Figure of Eight knot. This multi-purpose knot is invaluable for terminal rigs. The illustration details the tying and one must ensure only that both lengths of line are turned in the knot evenly to make a neat finish and alleviate strain on a single strand

The Figure of Eight loop, with the free end neatly whipped, can be a permanent feature of the reel line—ready to take any terminal rig finished with a link swivel

to be superior, in this instance, to the half-blood knot, and, of course, it accommodates all types of hooks. With 'spade-ends', the line should lead away from the rear of the spade, and with 'eyed' hooks, be passed through the eye. For security, always make at least six turns before tucking the free end of the line.

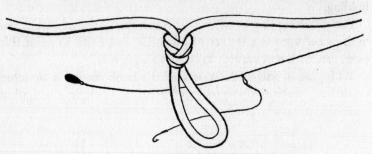

Tied in along the reel line, the Figure of Eight knot makes a quick and efficient 'soft' boom

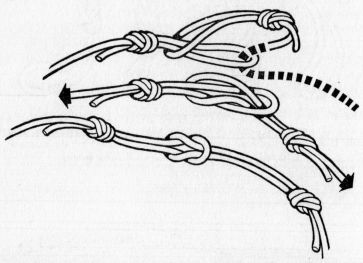

Joining Figure of Eight loops is simple and makes quite a safe purchase. Draw the loops gently but firmly away from each other and ensure that the strands of line lay evenly to form a reef knot at the centre. After fishing, of course, the loops are easily eased apart

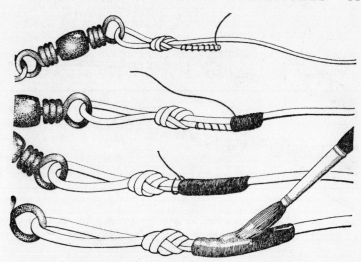

The Figure of Eight knot is my standard knot for making up nylon-covered wire traces—certainly I have more confidence in this knot than metal ferrules, which must fit exactly, or twisting the wire about itself and fusing the nylon with a flame. To make a neat finish, provide extra strength, and eliminate weed-drag, the free end of the wire should be whipped as shown and sealed with varnish. Clear nail varnish is ideal, and the handy bottle tucks away neatly in a corner of the tackle box for touching up whippings when necessary

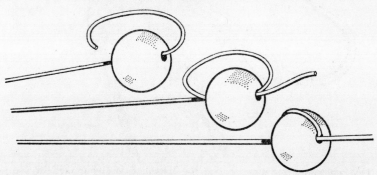

Sometimes, on a sliding leger rig, one wants to control the length of line in front of the lead. In such a case, the bead is hitched as shown when the tackle is made up. To move the bead, one merely slacks off the line on either side

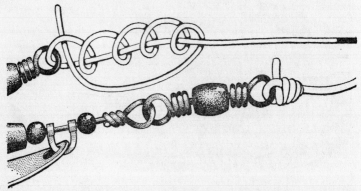

The Half-blood knot comes into its own for securing line to a swivel, or any item of terminal tackle with a straight eye

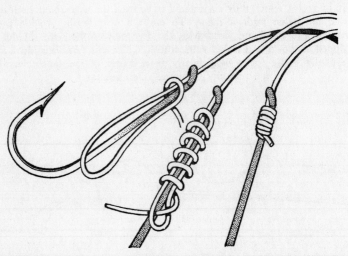

This whipping, sometimes called the 'Domhof' knot but used by commercial fishermen for hundreds of years, is the one I always use and I have never had cause to doubt it. However, some anglers claim that it is prone to work loose. To remove all risk of this, make at least six turns about the shank and daub the completed whipping with nail varnish

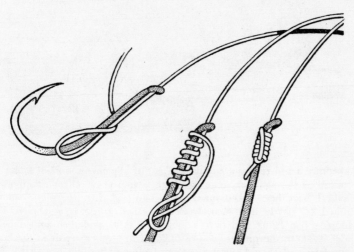

A similar but more easily tied form of whipping for turned-up eyes, turned-down eyes and spade-ends. This time, the turns start at the bottom of the shank and the free end is brought down into the loop and held while the reel line is drawn tight. In all knots and whippings the line must be drawn tight without a quick, jerking pull which could impart undue strain.

Again, the nail varnish treatment offers security

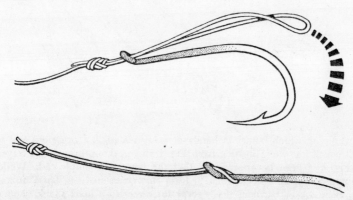

Back to the Figure of Eight loop for an emergency hook attachment. This attachment serves ideally when one wishes quickly to change hook sizes to come to terms with bites which bring no response

Sometimes a rod ring can be knocked out of alignment, worked loose, or even fall off through past abuse. While most anglers can effect a temporary repair, I have been asked many times how rod ring whippings can be finished off neatly and securely. The method I use is as shown, the whipping line being laid over a loop, tucked in, and then pulled back under itself. In the proper job—as opposed to a quick repair in the boat —the free end should not be cut until after varnishing has dried, for the then bristly strand is much easier to trim without risk of damage to the whipping

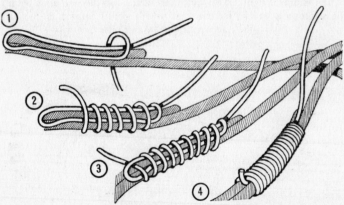

A whipping which comes in handy in many sea-angling situations and is well worth knowing. Starting from Fig. 1 and working through the stages to Fig. 4, it can be appreciated that the tying is a simple task. While whippings can be used as such to form emergency loops in boats' ropes, etc, their use in terminal rigs, except for direct to a hook shank, should be restricted to backing up a knot, rather than as a definite holding feature. Where whippings are used, always make as many turns as possible and certainly a minimum of six

Acknowledgements

A writer, particularly one concerned with a specialised field, invariably owes much to all manner of people for his progress. Each new book is the sum of what he learns by his own account and by gleaning, often subconsciously, from other people. Sometimes these people are themselves unable to write, but have a brilliance in their particular field which is passed on to the writer by impression, and sometimes fellow writers make points so well that these, too, are imprinted in the mind. After a time the origins become obscure, forming part of a personal fund of knowledge which contributes to one's skill.

To the many people who have provided something, I would like to take this opportunity to express my gratitude, but I would particularly thank E. O. Z. Wade, who has contributed much to my knowledge of fish, and Barrie Welham, who has influenced my fishing over the years with advice on many facets of casting. Also Richard Walker, who started me looking into the subject more deeply. Much of what I have learned from these people is in this book.

On more tangible grounds, I acknowledge thanks to John Ingham, of *Angler's Mail*, for permission to reproduce several of my drawings which have appeared in that newspaper in recent years.

DAVID CARL FORBES

Index

Float rig, 103
Floats, 108
Flounder, 11, 74, 121–3: physical
  characteristics, 122; habitat,
  121–2; record weight for, 123
Fluke, or white fluke, *see* Flounder

Groin protector, 76–7: importance
  as an accessory, 76–7
Gurnard, 129, 140

Haddock, 123–4, 127: location of,
  123; physical characteristics,
  123–4; diet of, 124; record weight
  for, 124
Hake, 124–5: physical characteristics, 124–5; diet of, 125
Halibut, 126–7: location of, 126;
  record weight for, 127; physical
  characteristics, 127
Harness lugs, for harness use, 30
Herrings, as bait, 52, 117, 125,
  136–7, 140, 143
Hooks: identification of, 38–9;
  different styles of, 39; fine-wire
  long-shanked, 39–40; forged steel
  barbed, 39–40; 'eye' or 'spade-end'
  of, 39, 146; design and length of
  shank of, 39; importance of scal-
  ing to bait, 40; to test, 40–1;
  forged stainless steel, 41; guide to
  sizes of, 41

Illingworth, Alfred Holden, 22:
  reel invented by, 22

Jenkins, J. Travis, 127, 129: Works,
  Fishes of the British Isles, 127q.,
  129q.

Knots, 144–50: double loop, 145;
  double figure of eight, 145–7, 149;
  blood blight, 145; half blood,
  145–6, 148; 'Domhof', 148

'Lay-back' casting method, 68–70
Leads: Jardine special, 43; pear, 43,
  65; Capta, 43; drilled bullet, 43,
  108; sheet, 43, 108; split shot, 43;
  spiked torpedo, 43; barrel, 108
Legering, 12
Line: breaking strain of, 18–19,
  23–4, 31–2, 34, 61–2; types of,
  35–6
Ling, 73, 127–9: location of, 128;
  physical characteristics, 127–8;
  diet of, 129; record weight for, 129
Littlehampton, concentration of
  Black bream at, 115
Lobster, 117, 127
Lugworm, as bait, 49, 100, 109
Lures, 53–4, 80–1, 109: importance
  of shape of, 54
Lusitania, 128

Mackerel, 12, 81, 105–6, 113, 117,
  125, 129–30, 137, 140: as baits
  for tope, 52, 84, 88; as bait for
  conger eel, 88; tackle for, 106;
  location, 129–30; physical characteristics, 130; record weight for,
  130
Maggots, 47
Mako, 98, 137–8, 140: physical
  characteristics, 137; location, 137;
  record weight for, 137–8
Moncrieff, Leslie, 56–8, 68, 70
Mullet, 103, 107: bait for, 103–4;
  suitable tackle, 103; catching and
  landing, 104–5
Mullet, grey, 130–3: location, 130;
  physical characteristics, 131–2;
  nature, 132; diet of, 132; record
  weight for, 133; best site for
  catching, 133
Mussel, as bait, 52
'Murderers', 80

Nottingham reel, 34
Nylon monofilament line, 35–6, 64,
  66, 82, 144

Paternosters, 57
Pilchards, as bait, 52, 126, 136–7